For Brenda,
Hope you like the book.
– En Zo

Brenda –
En Joy
Martha Frankel

Brenda
Hope you...
XO

MY BODY, MY WORDS
a collection of bodies

For Brenda
Your daughter
is a joy!
Kitty Sher

For Brenda,
(Laurie's mother)
with very best wishes!
Anju Thuma

Brenda,
Thank you
so much
for your support

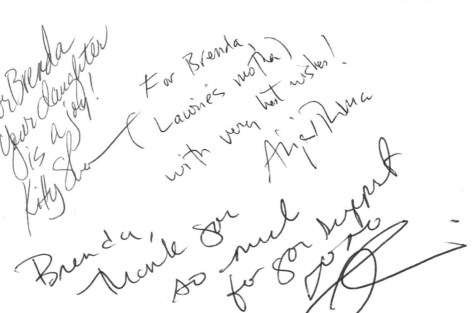

Edited by Loren Kleinman and Amye Archer
with an Introduction by Martha Frankel

To Brenda –
Tell your story!
xo Kathn McKitty Sher

ISBN: 978-1-945917-34-9

Printed in the United States of America

Cover Art: Marisa Gershenhorn

"Making other books jealous since 2004"

Big Table Publishing Company
Boston, MA
www.bigtablepublishing.com

For Samantha and Penelope—Thank you for always seeing the beauty in me.
~ Amye (Mommy)

For Joseph—For loving my body in sickness and in health.
~ Loren

Table of Contents

MY BODY, MY WORDS

a collection of bodies

Edited by Loren Kleinman and Amye Archer
with an Introduction by Martha Frankel

Introduction

Whenever someone takes my photo, right before they click the shutter, I say, "hey, make me look…" and everyone, *everyone*, from the photographer to a waiter walking by to the other people in the shot, chimes in and says "*thin*." I talk over them. "*Smart*," I say loudly. "Make me look smart." And people laugh nervously. Because in the battle of smart vs thin, thin wins every day of the week.

We'd pretty much trade anything, including health and sanity, for thin. It's our one true religion.

In my house growing up, we were loud, and we were Jewish, and food was a way to say I love you. I've heard from far too many friends over the years that it was also a way to punish you, but that wasn't my experience. My mother loved my sister Helene and I unconditionally. She stood at the stove and listened to us and would encourage us to dance and be sassy and helped us create versions of ourselves that felt zany and bold. She never criticized the way we looked, never told us to be anything but what we were. My aunts would come over for their "diet lunches"—BLTs on white bread with a schmear of mayo. But they liked their zaftig bosoms and would often implore everyone to eat more.

When my father died, just after I hit puberty, I started waging war with my body. I willed it to be thinner, less curvy, not so damn fleshy. My breasts grew quickly and seemed disproportionate to the rest of me. If I had known about binding I would have tried it. Instead I wore bras that were a few sizes too tight, flattening me and making me look more like a linebacker than a ballerina. I wanted to go back to that time before we lost him, when I was a little girl and there really were no monsters hiding in the shadows. Clearly those days were gone.

A few years later I began waging war another way. Now my tops barely covered my breasts; my lidded eyes dared you to make a comment or an assumption. I felt completely disconnected from myself, and was often surprised when I saw my reflection. That person in those clothes seemed everything I wasn't—in charge, unafraid. That girl looked so at ease it took my breath away.

It's really no surprise then that my first published story, in the original *DETAILS* magazine, was about my breast reduction surgery.

My body and I had come to an odd detente, but when people began posting old photos on Facebook every Thursday, I had a revelation. I gathered pictures from 10, 20, 30 years ago. I looked at them and had to admit I looked fine, sometimes even great. It was like discovering your alarm radio was also transmitting with aliens. Because I still remembered how I felt when I waited for that shutter to click. I was worried—about my weight, or the way my hair looked, or the way my clothes bunched up around my belly. I remember sucking in, or jutting forward, or turning to the right, to hide an overbite that now seems charming. I was a mess of insecurities, wrapped in a patina of shiny ribbon.

Once, at a diner near my home in Woodstock, NY, I ordered a vanilla malted. The waitress paused, pen mid-air, to look directly at my legs. She didn't even try to hide her curiosity. When she deemed my thighs small enough, she nodded and wrote the order on her pad. I could barely sip that sweet concoction when she brought it. Being judged has that effect.

But I was a judger, too. I would look women up and down surreptitiously, and make these comparisons. Ok, her hair is better, but my waist is smaller. Sure, she's thinner, but I'm smarter. Or worse, Yes, she's smarter, but I'm thinner!

It was only when I started writing professionally that I began to have hours where I didn't even notice my body, and when I did, I would smile with understanding. It was just a vessel, meant to house my brain. Anything more was a gift.

Our relationship to our bodies, our hoping that things will be better if only… is the bane of many people I know. I was about to say *many women I know*, but men have proven to be equally obsessed and insecure.

The stories in this collection are at once heartbreaking and uplifting. We are shaped by many things, and while our relationship to our stomachs might be a defining one, there are many others. The off-hand thing an adult says to a teen. The way someone looks at you when you're meant to be unselfconscious. The way we think lovers are judging us. The way we judge lovers! Lights on? Lights off? Oh please don't let them touch my love handles. All of this determines how we feel about our bodies.

There are drugs and periods and infidelities in *My Body, My Words*. There is sadness and strength, addiction and romance. There are young people looking forward, and older ones looking back. There's too big, and even bigger. There's too thin, but not as much. There's thighs that jiggle and stretch marks galore. And of course, there's ice cream. Thank heavens there's ice cream!

In short, this book contains all the things that shape us. Kathleen Harris' relationship to her body is filtered thru her Irish Catholic guilt. Kitty Sheehan's self-image was shaped by *Seventeen* Magazine. Monique Antonette Lewis reclaims the blackness of her beautiful hair with the help of India Arie, Amel Larrieux, Lauryn Hill and Erykah Badu. Heidi Stuber sees her life story through her weight and body-fat measurements. Eloisa Perez-Lozano constantly compares herself to the Latina ideal, Jim Warner examines body image and weight loss through the eyes of a former lover, and Eve Fox is a preteen when a young man begins to make her and her best friend uncomfortable in the pool.

What we come away with is the whole mess of being human, the little slights and the major victories, the weight our bodies carry and the weight we put on them. Enjoy.

Martha Frankel, 2018
Woodstock, NY

"Can I be blamed for wanting a real body, to put my arms around?
Without it I too am disembodied."

~ Margaret Atwood, *The Handmaid's Tale*

"You are imperfect, permanently and inevitably flawed.
And you are beautiful."

~ Amy Bloom

THE BODY IS A POEM
Loren Kleinman

I'm beautiful.

I say it under the dim bathroom light: I. Am. Beautiful.

I take solace in the light on my face. I take solace in the light on my skin, on the fat that creases and bulges. I hold my stomach in my hands, squish and squash my love handles. Rub my flank, along the length of ribs, down to the pelvis. The stretch marks are lines on paper; they're crooked and scribbled on my skin. Each line and *L*, elongated.

I love my body. Sometimes I love it more, and sometimes I love it less. And in the past, I've doubted my temple. I've fed it horrible things like stress and butter and beer.

I've hated it, slapped my stomach in front of the mirror, left red marks and scratches. I've made faces at my overweight self: pig-nosed wide mouthed. I've even cut my thighs, made new lines, new *LJ/////s*.

Not today.

I remember where I started: I am beautiful. I put the magazine down. I stop reading the lines about how to fit in my jeans better (or for that matter, how to fit in). I tell the page it doesn't know me like I know me. I tell myself I'm not a model. I tell myself the models are not even models. They are made of wood held together by string.

I stand in front of the mirror. My skin is a white sheet of paper. My eyes are two buckets of brown dirt. I don't cry anymore over my curves. I feed my body apples, pears, and squash. I feed it squats and walks. I wash the sweat off from my workout in a warm, lavender-scented shower. The shower is a lake from a dream I had.

I don't body-shame myself. I don't let others body shame me

either. I'm responsible for how I see myself in this world, in this long and wide world of hurtful words and scams of the heart.

Go now. This is not a body of hate. This body does not hate itself. There's nothing here to consume, but love. Self-sabotage is a hand that does not hurt me anymore. My body sings me to sleep. My body is ground, gravel, twigs, and brambles.

My feet dangle from the bed. I examine the cracked skin, the dried patches on the tops of my toes. I see my legs, freckled and chubby, against the cat's back. I rub my arms, the stretched skin, too.

I pull my messy hair back in a bun and sigh deep and slow. The room is quiet.

The bathroom mirror is quiet. There is no sound—only my heart, gentle and warm, and it says, *Thank you for loving me again.* And my fingers rest on my chest. They can hear the sound of my heart.

I push myself off the bed and look in the long, wooden framed mirror. All those spots. All those scars and scabs. All those dimples in the thigh.

It's all a poem to me.

OBJECT PERMANENCE

Amye Archer

Object Permanence: the stage of childhood development in which a baby learns that what he or she cannot see still exists.

It is dark. The summer is ending, but we can still taste her on our tongues. Twenty beers between us have made you hungry for me. We roll through ten years of married sex like we are still in month one. Everything is unzipped, my dress, your pants, even our mouths-as we say things to one another in the dark we wouldn't dare to whisper in the light. My breasts are soft under your palms and lips. Your hands are rough, but my body contours to them with familiarity. "You should be worshipped," you slur into my neck. I cling to you tightly, enveloping your thin body between my arms, and I hold on. I narrow myself, sucking in my belly, squeezing my hips together, our bed is small, and I need to make room for the girl next to us.

"I have loved you since I was a boy," you tell me. The girl hears it too. This girl, the one on her back with our moans in her ears is always with me. She is 265 pounds, she is desperate and wide. She is 24 forever. She thinks her husband loves her because he allows her to exist as fat. She thinks sex is about his orgasm, not her beauty. She won't leave a bad marriage, she won't find a new job, and she won't write books or birth children. She will live in 2002 forever. She hears you talking from fifteen years ago.

Hears the promises you make, the way love should sound, but she can't reach you. She can only reach me.

Twenty beers between us have left an awful ache the next morning. The sun burns through us. You rise first, still naked, still smooth and hard all at once. You walk across wood floors you have laid, held together by walls you have built, and I watch through one heavy eye the grace you would never admit to having in your step.

You ask about my Needs-aspirin, water, food. The girl between us is confused by this care. She wants to run to you. To care for you. Her inflated body begins to rise. I throw my arm across her belly, pull her back into the bed with me and whisper: "It's okay. Let him do this.

LONG TREK
Ryan K. Sallans

Light begins to stream through my eyelids, serving as Mother Nature's alarm clock. Usually, I welcome this gradual form of awakening in the morning, but not when I am staying on the west coast, where the sun likes to make its appearance at the ungodly hour of four-fifty in the morning. As I arouse, I notice the chorus of chirps coming from the treetops that surround the valley. I remain tucked away in my dome tent, burritoed inside my sleeping bag that serves as my place of warmth and comfort, while surrounded by the unknowns of nature in the wilderness.

Over the past five years I've taken advantage of the summer months, when the snow breaks away from the mountaintops and drips water into the streams and lakes below. These months create the small window of time that allows me to strap a large pack onto my back and climb atop cliffs to see the wide-spanning vista views and walk through the valleys filled with wildflowers and ground dwelling marmots. I've always loved nature, even as a child, but it has only been the last few years that I've also appreciated the body that is carrying me from one place to the other.

While today, I walk through nature and the rest of the world as a middle-aged man, I was born assigned female and socially reared as a woman in a small, conservative, farming town in Nebraska. I was taught that to be accepted I should wear certain clothes, style my hair (which should be long), and apply make-up to my face so that I would look pretty, *the boys like you better if you look pretty*. While these were lessons I was taught, I didn't follow the instructions very well . . . actually . . . I mostly avoided them.

As I entered college, the discomfort that came with being in an unfamiliar place and around people I was just getting to know, led me to internalize all the messaging I received growing up. I felt completely out-of-place, and believed that if I changed my appearance, I would feel better and be accepted. Before class, I would awkwardly put on make-up. On the weekends, I would have my sister, who was in beauty school, put highlights in my hair. And when I went shopping, I would force myself to not go into the guy's section to buy my clothing, I felt I should wear women's clothing when attempting to shyly flirt with the boys I met. But even after all of that, I still felt uncomfortable in my skin.

The fix, I decided, was to become skinny. A task I felt was near to impossible for what I perceived as my larger-framed body. As the months passed by, my body whittled away to the point that I nearly died. The sicker I became, the more I realized that my behaviors were not relieving my discomfort, they were only making it worse. By age 23, I believed I was broken and unable to heal or find a place in life where I felt okay with being me. Through exploring sexuality, which was a feat in-and-of-itself, I first recognized my attraction and attachment to women and came out as lesbian. After eight months in the LGBT community, I discovered that I was transgender. Five months later, at age 25 in 2005, I began my transition from female-to-male in Lincoln, Nebraska.

Over the first two years of my transition, I had a monthly ritual where I would take different posed pictures of my body. Each time I flipped the pages of my calendar that hung in my office, I knew it was time to take photos, documenting the changes in my shape and form due to my weekly injections of testosterone that were soaked up by my muscles, and surgical procedures that helped align my body with my mind. When I was anorexic, I also took pictures of my body, but the ones during my transition were different from the past. I no longer hid my face or looked blankly into the camera, hollow eyes and hollow shell.

Now, as the camera shutter clicked, images were captured of a torso shifting from hour glass to v-shape, a face shifting from oval to h-shaped with hair speckling the neck and chin, and a back with broadening shoulders as bookends. I documented every little change that took place. I documented how the two scars changed that ran on the underside of my chest where a surgeon made incisions to remove the breast that were never welcomed guests on my body.

I did this to help me understand how my transgender identity was separate from my body image, and how they also influenced each other. The photos were there to help me discover the point where negative body image ends and life begins.

As the months continued to pass, I slowly began to feel like I was moving into a home that wanted me to be its guest and tenant. An odd feeling and a complex process that I will forever be thankful for. I wish I could say everything is perfect now, but even with hormones and surgery, the inner voices that started in early childhood have still staked claim in my mind. These voices get louder when the online world starts to share their own thoughts about who I am and how I look. I am hoping that at some point, I can just say, "Fuck it." But it is difficult to be judged by appearance and perceptions, and have that reinforced by others seeking meaning through targeted attacks.

My place for escape has become the wilderness. The animals, trees, and other hikers are not out there to judge. We are all out there to take in the great beauty of nature, and to challenge our bodies and minds. If you are out for more than two days, you smell, your hair is greasy, dirt lines form in the creases of your skin and smudges your face, but you don't care, nor do the others that you come across on the trail. There are no mirrors, the streams and lakes serve as the places where you dip a washcloth and run it over your skin at night, and a hat presses down the tangles of your hair. Being freed from reflections, allows your thoughts to be free of judgment.

In the wilderness, I take my sweat-soaked shirt off, letting the sun's rays dry the moisture beaded on my skin, warming the surface in the process. As other hikers trek by, I wave at them; they either wave back or give a nod depending on how tired they are from their day's trip. They see me as just a guy out in the wilderness, and so do I, freeing me from labels and the voices.

MY BODY IS NOT MY OWN
Jason Fjord

The first time I learned my body was not my own was when another little boy lifted up my pretty little dress and I screamed. I got yelled at for screaming while he sat in the corner, giggling to himself.

The second time I learned my body was not my own was when I was getting my first conscious vaccine. I screamed and screamed and kicked and punched. But instead of explaining it to me, my male doctor held me down and my dad didn't say a word.

The third day I learned my body was not my own was when I went to my grandmother's house and I was forced to kiss and hug her hello and goodbye. She slapped my butt and squeezed my butt, and even though I cried on the way home I was told to suck it up, because that was just what people her age did.

The fourth day I learned my body was not my own was when my dad died and my uncle pulled me onto his lap to make me stop crying, even though I didn't want him to touch me. I learned I wasn't allowed to be weak, to cry, to express anything besides pure unadulterated joy.

The fifth day I learned my body was not my own I was 11 and 6 men decided that fucking the faggot that liked girls was top priority. I learned then that my body is a tool to be used by others at will, regardless of whatever pain I might be in, because simply by existing I am asking for it.

The sixth day I learned my body was not my own was when I was manipulated into showing myself online because I thought I was only a tool to be used by others.

And on the seventh day I learned my body was mine to take back. My body has been stolen from me. By my family, my abusers, my rapists, by the society I live in that tells me my gender is between my legs and not my ears.

My body is my own. I have fought for it. I have cried for it. I have bled for it. I have become my worst nightmare to protect it. I have lied for it. I have died for it. I was born for this.

My body is my own. I will fight for it. I will cry for it. I will bleed for it. I will become my brightest and farthest dream for it. I will lie for it. I will die for it. I was not made for this. I made myself for this.

My body is my own. It deserves the best I can give it. The best care, the best food, the best sleep, the best emotions, the best expressions.

My body deserves the Pride everyone else has.

I deserve Pride because that is the only thing that cannot be taken from me. My body has seen war.

My body will have its medals, and its purple hearts. My body is my own because I made it so.

MOSTLY FEMALE
E.R. Zhang

My pen hovers over the two boxes.
Male. Female.
Female, I guess.

My friend checks "female" without a second thought, and moves to the next question. She's never questioned whether this is who she is, whether this is who she's supposed to be. She doesn't know what it feels like to not know.

It's not about wanting to be a man. It's not about hating the body I've been given, or wishing I were thinner, taller, or prettier. This body is like the pair of pants I bought last week. They fit perfectly in the changing room, but the large lunch I had now makes them too tight. A week from now, when I put them on again, they're too loose because I've been sick with stomach flu. Two weeks from now, they're a perfect fit again. I love them until I gain two pounds on vacation and then they don't fit again.

This body is like the lock that sticks at random, even when I oil it. It refuses to open on some days, and slides open on others. It's not causing enough trouble that I want a new one. I wish it would behave for a bit. And when I think I've oiled it enough and it hasn't stuck for months, I find it inoperable when it's pouring; I'm wet and stuck outside.

This body is the old CD I play in the car that skips on track 3, 7, and 19. (Sometimes 5, 14, and 24 if it's feeling rebellious.) It's annoying when I'm trying to sing along, but then again, it has all my beloved songs, and when it plays fine, I forget about replacing the CD.

It's my favorite soda, but the recipe changes and it doesn't taste the way it did when I was three years old.

28

It's like coming in fourth, a half point behind third, and I can't exactly claim to be as good as the best, but I was *that* close.

It's an outsider, a pretender masquerading as someone else.

For months at a time, this is *just* a body. Not my body, but a vessel on loan. It doesn't fit perfectly, but it's as close as I can get. One size up is too big. One size down is too small. I'm taking in the corners, making my own darts to make it better. When I'm done with alterations, I'm ripping out the tag they stuck on at birth and sewing my own onto it instead.

Someone I don't know will say, "What are you wearing? I've never heard of that designer before."

***

I relish anonymous surveys. I can check 'male' without paranoia. Sometimes, anonymous online surveys even have the 'other' option. That one's the best. That one's *mostly* me. But for now, I check "female", only because I don't want to stir up trouble.

I wake up and it's a boy day.

I wake up and it's a girl day.

I wake up and it's a day.

I wake up and it's day.

IN PROGRESS

Taylor Dibble

When the question "How do you identify yourself?" is shot up in
class from a starting pistol the class is off to the races.
The scratching of pens gathers
together in my ears like a pack. Did
you know wolves howl at the moon
to find each other?
But I cry at
night because I
can't find
myself. I am a
deserted island
full of faceless
dolls.
A museum with all the exhibits under construction.
A link in a broken chain
and thrown away pizza
crust. I am self-baptized
in a dirty bathtub.
Our bodies are temples but what if we no
longer feel like the owner? Wrapped in a
sheet of flesh that doesn't quite fit right.
Too baggy in the chest or too tight on the shoulders.
Always in the hand-me-downs of someone we are supposed to
become.

***

There's a guitar that sits in the corner of my bedroom and I
have no idea how to play it. I spend more time staring at the
curves than learning how to pluck the strings.
I wonder if you played me correctly I would finally sound beautiful.
I know I talk a lot, it's only because I don't want to forget what I
sound like.
I am medically overweight but I know those extra pounds come from
the grenade clipped to my tongue.
I'm told poets have switchblade words and lately my mouth has been
so full of my own blood I've begun to believe that.
A poet once told me they used to get "rapper hands" when they
performed and that it's completely normal.
But the only wrapping I do is at Christmas, boxing up fake
smiles for family members. A season of giving, but lately all
everyone does is take.
He used to look at me like a lion does before it pounces on its prey.
He used to think that if he set the table he could put
whatever he wanted on the plate. There he was, grinning,
teeth bared.
Did you ever think twice before you swallowed me whole?
I have given away parts of myself I am still
searching for to get back. The small of my
back was in the flash of a camera.
My dignity and dependence had been camping out in the hum of a
fluorescent light.
Making love to the memories of when I considered myself as a good
person has become habit. I'm a nymphomaniac of defeat.
A poet once told me that I'm not the monster I make myself out to
be in my poems and in two short days I have started to believe him.
Because my suicide date was set for May, but now the name May
has a place in my heart. For giving me another reason to live,
for giving me
eight more
reasons to
live, for

31

giving me
endless
reasons to
live.
I am going to be me no matter what metaphor I string to myself
so I better make it a good one.

A TIMELINE OF HUMAN

FEMALE DEVELOPMENT

Kathleen McKitty Harris

1970: On the night that I am born, Janis Joplin performs at what will be her last live concert. She wails to a sold-out crowd at Boston's Harvard Stadium, while my twenty-two-year-old mother endures contractions in a Manhattan hospital. I am too large to make safe passage through my mother's narrow pelvis. She—we—are not progressing. My mother is given pentothal, and wheeled to the delivery room, where I finally emerge. A big, healthy girl, the obstetrician tells my mother afterwards. I weigh 8 pounds, 2 ounces.

1973: My mother tells me that I can't eat the candy in the box that says AYDS. When my mother talks on the phone, I hide and eat chocolate chips from a torn yellow bag. I watch the phone cord tense and bob while she paces in the kitchen, and gorge until it stops moving. I know that what I am doing is wrong. I am three.

1974: My father's two older sisters, once slim in their youth, are now obese. Their stomachs hang past their knees. Sacks of fat hang on their shin bones. One of my aunts wears a woolen poncho in the winter, because no store sells a coat large enough to fit her. They are soft, warm and kind, and I adore them. Other people whisper when they leave the room.

1976: During the bicentennial, girls across America portray Betsy Ross at school pageants. They sit silent, miming sewing motions, and decorate the stage. Boys are given the role of George Washington in these plays. They win the Revolutionary War. They recite important speeches and become the first president of the United States.

1977: A family friend is anorexic and bulimic: words I don't yet know, but nod at while reading their definitions years later. Her daily intake consists of one pack of Viceroys, one lettuce leaf and one slice of Boars Head bologna arranged on a fluted paper plate. She vomits sometimes in a small powder room off the kitchen.

1978: While watching a Betamax tape of *Grease* at a sleepover, I am confused by Olivia Newton-John's change of outfit and hairstyle in the final scene. The other girls at the party get up and dance to the musical number in their tube socks and nightgowns. I feel betrayed.

1979: I find a rolled-up *Playboy* in a friend's bathroom. I lock the door and turn the pages. I stare at angora sweaters, feathered hair, glossy lips, splayed-open legs. I am nine, and I want to look like Kate Jackson in a cowl-neck sweater, like Suzanne Somers in piped shorts, like Farrah Fawcett in anything. I can't look away.

1981: Our Catholic grammar school in Queens has marble floors, saints and saviors on pedestals and crosses, and stone lintels above the doors, carved with letters that spell BOYS and GIRLS. A nun teaches us sex education, with the aid of jumpy filmstrips and line drawings of genitalia on overhead projectors. We are separated from the boys in our class for this unit of study. A girl raises her hand and asks how the nun knows the size of a penis if she's never seen one. The nun doesn't answer.

1982: I gain weight during puberty. I'm a latchkey kid, and am home alone for several hours before my parents return from work. My parents have recently told me that they plan to separate. I quell my anxiety by eating Cool Whip from the fridge. Before my mother comes home, I sculpt the remaining synthetic whipped topping into a froth with a spoon, hoping to camouflage the emptiness.

1983: We move from Queens to Connecticut. I have always worn a Catholic school uniform, and know nothing about designer labels. My parents can't afford to buy me expensive clothes, but I beg for an Izod polo shirt. My mother asks why a similar shirt from Caldor can't pass muster. "Izod has an alligator and Caldor's has a raccoon—they're both wild animals. What's the difference?" I try on the cheaper shirt, and my mother frowns at the tight swath of pique cotton pulled across my fleshy stomach. "Don't tuck it in like that," she says. "It looks too tight across"—she points and waggles her index finger—"THAT area. Blouse it. It looks better."

1984: I see an ad for a fat camp in Massachusetts, and tell my parents that I want to go. I meet ten-year old bulimics, boys who weigh 300 pounds, girls who cry in the dark about the abuse they suffer at home. I meet kids who are wounded and scarred, who use food as self-flagellation and solace. A boy at camp asks me to go out with him, and holds my hand. I tell him that I don't want to kiss him, I don't want to do anything with him. I don't want my first sexual anything to be imprinted with the memory of this place.

1985: A high school senior walks past me in an empty hallway and tweaks my right breast. I start wearing my Limited shaker sweater sleeves over my clenched fists. It makes me feel smaller.

1986: I get my driver's license. I lie about my weight on the DMV form. My lie is laminated and heat-sealed.

1987: I take step aerobics at the YMCA with a friend. She produces a box of laxatives from her purse after class.

1988: I try on prom dresses at Macy's. I am a size 16, but cling to the fantasy that I am still a size 13—the last number in the juniors' section. The only dress that fits makes me look like a salmon jacquard couch. At the prom, I stand awkwardly with my date for photos. His hands rest on my hips while we pose. I disassociate from the ripples of flesh beneath the lace and satin.

1990: I study abroad in Europe, and travel to Spain during a school holiday with a female friend. We plan to visit a Roman aqueduct named the Pont del Diable—"The Devil's Bridge"—in Tarragona. The site is remote. We hike a mile into the wilderness and find the ancient structure. We are alone, save for a thirty something man standing nearby. He approaches us, holding his stiff penis above the waistband of his sweatpants. "AmerEEkahn girls, AmerEEkahn girls," he moans, while jerking off. We run back to the main road, and drink cervezas at a roadside bar until our hands stop shaking.

1991: My aunt dies suddenly. My mother has to select the outfit that the undertaker will dress her in, and can find nothing to fit her corpse. I lose thirty pounds that year.

1992: I graduate from college and move to Manhattan. I am whistled at, hissed at, propositioned on the street. Men tell me to smile when I pay for coffee or cigarettes. I am groped on the 4 train, flashed on the 6 train, prodded by gabardine-clad hard-ons on the 2 train.

1994: I work for a magazine publisher in Manhattan. Our art department digitally enhances the pictures of young models. I try to make myself vomit in empty office bathrooms after eating bad office birthday party cake. My body refuses to comply.

1995: My boyfriend proposes. I think I am too fat to be an attractive bride. I weigh 131 pounds. I try the Cabbage Soup Diet, the Slim-Fast

Diet, the Diet-Coke-Marlboro-Lights-and Fat-Free-Muffins Diet. I eat only oranges one day, red meat the next. On my wedding day, I weigh 127 pounds.

1998: I want liposuction. I weigh 137 pounds. I take some freelance writing jobs to pay for the surgery. I write ad copy for clothing stores that tout Lycra and slim-fit khakis. A few months later, I have the procedure. I ask to see the fat that has been extracted. The nurse frowns. She says it's unsightly, like thick carrot soup. I wouldn't want to see that, she says. They throw that part of me away.

2001: I am seven months pregnant. My husband's boss greets me at a party: "Hey, fat girl."

2004: I see a nutritionist because we want to have another child, but I'm worried about gaining weight. She suggests eating string cheese to satiate hunger between meals. I chew on flaccid cheese sticks in the light of my open refrigerator.

2006: I can't lose the weight I've gained since my second pregnancy. I weigh 164 pounds. My husband motions for me to sit in his lap, but I worry that he will feel the full weight of my body and no longer be attracted to it, to me. I sit beside him on the couch instead. We don't touch.

2016: I still suck in my stomach when my husband and I have sex, when we spoon in bed, whenever his hand grazes my belly or side. The muscle contraction is involuntary. He says I'm beautiful, sexy, and goddess-like. I roll my eyes. He sighs.

2017: My father never liked Janis Joplin. She was too loud, he says. Too much. I play my mother's 1970 vinyl LP of *Pearl*, and listen to "Me and Bobby McGee" in the dark.

THE MEASURE OF A GIRL

Kitty Sheehan

My ideal body image was dictated to me by Enid A. Haupt.

Haupt was the editor-in-chief of *Seventeen* magazine from 1953-1970: catching my formative years at the tail end of her reign. I see you doing the math. Don't worry; we'll do it later. Keep reading. Enid was the daughter of Moses Annenberg, who created a publishing empire starting in 1922 with *The Daily Racing Form*. The Annenberg family's holdings included radio and television stations, the Philadelphia Inquirer, the Philadelphia Daily News and TV Guide, which Enid's brother Walter Annenberg founded in 1953.

Walter gave his sister a job as publisher, editor and editor-in-chief of *Seventeen* magazine, another family publication.

"Walter foisted the editorship on me when he was terminating a lady who had become a great nuisance," Mrs. Haupt said. "I knew nothing about running a magazine, but my brother said, 'You can bring culture to the average working person who has not had your advantages.'"

That'd be me.

Seventeen began in 1944, with a mission to inspire teen girls to become serious workers and citizens. Helen Valentine, the first editor, provided young women with working female role models and information about their development. When it became obvious that teen girls were consumers of popular culture, *Seventeen's* focus shifted to fashion and beauty, which could be bought and sold. Helen Valentine was now Walter Annenberg's "great nuisance," as she believed in presenting a well-rounded image for young girls to aspire to, not just a fashion ideal.

Scram, Helen. Your services are no longer needed.

38

Growing up in the small Iowa town of Carroll, *Seventeen* was my bible. During the summer after 9th grade, I checked out all the old issues in existence at the Carroll Public Library—reading back to 1950, intrigued with every patent leather purse, plaid skirt and London Fog raincoat. No detail escaped my microscopic inspection.

What was I looking for? I wanted to be like these impossibly cute and skinny girls who wore the perfect clothes while they rode bikes in the city, held slides up to the window in science classrooms, made fondue for their boyfriends, or lounged on the steps of museums.

My DIY instructions came via the ad copy in these pages, shaped by Enid Haupt. Here's where I learned how and what I should be. Check out these examples from the February 1970 issue.

Eventually, he'll get to your feet.
It's only a matter of time.
So be sure your feet can finish whatever your face starts.
In Lady Bostonians, you're his kind of girl. With it from head to toe.
Get a pair quick, before he finds out there's more to you than just your pretty face.
Lady Bostonians
Shoes that communicate.

Lesson: OK, clearly, every man who looks at me will give me the once-over. He'll start at my head. I think. But my feet need to be ready, at all times. The Lady Bostonians in the ad are just how they sound. Loafers with tassels. Tassels talk, I guess. I need some, quick. I need to be "with it." No one, especially me, wants to be without it. That is not my deal. My deal is to be his kind of girl. Please, let me be his kind of girl.

WE MAKE PANTYHOSE FOR MEN.
(Legmen.)
They're worn by women, of course. But they're really made for men.

Men who are sensitive to the beat of youthful legs.
Who are turned-off by tired legs. Legmen. They're a special
breed.
So are our pantyhose. Roman Stripe pantyhose. From Alba-
Waldensian.
Sheer support and stretch pantyhose. In many mood-
flattering fashion colors.
Wear Roman Stripe pantyhose. Legmen will notice.
And they'll appreciate your thoughtfulness.

Do I know any legmen? I wonder if that senior boy I'm crushing on is sensitive to the beat of youthful legs. How to tell? Are my legs youthful enough? God, I hope so. They're rarely tired legs, since I hate running. They aren't haggard legs, like older girls drag around. So that's a win for me. And now I can flatter my mood with fashion colors. I'm 14, so my mood needs some flattering. I just have to figure out how to do this with pantyhose, which usually don't flatter anything on me. It seems in order to appear thoughtful, I need to wear them. Is thoughtfulness the same as beauty? Beauty seems more important. When did thoughtfulness become a thing? Shit. And just who is this Alba-Waldensian?

Peaches & Gleam! Pinking Sheer! Lo-Cal Coral!
What's now, Wonderchild?
'PlexiGloss Pales'
7 new un-lipsticks that shine wild. Color soft. (loaded with
plex-appeal!)
What's a nice girl like you doing in a glaze like this? Looking
spiffy, that's what. Smashy. Your lips all paled-down color
and glossed-up shine.
Very glissy. Very kissy.
4 new super-super sheers. 3 new super-pale frost-things.
Get your hot little hands on them. Oh, wow. Now.
Natural Wonder by Revlon
For pretty young things.

Now. Everything is *now*. And wild. Being sexy in 1970 is suddenly as important as being "good" and waaaaaay more important than being smart. No lipstick is ever marketed to make you look smarter, just more kissable. Hence, being kissable is better than being smart. It's simple, really. But where to start? How to get "smashy" lips? The crucial thing is a balance between pale and glossy. This is the opposite of my mother's matte red lips. Which one of us is more kissy? I'm younger, so I think it must be me.

My mother certainly never talked to me about any of this. Her generation of women came of age post-WW2, and they were supposed to keep a perfect house and lust after dishwashers. Since she did neither, she was conflicted.

Outside, in the real world, Gloria Steinem encouraged women to burn their bras. Not one mention in my magazine pages of bras burning. I paid for my bra with my own money, mostly so the mean girls would stop making fun of my flat chest in gym class. Setting it on fire held no meaning for me. The secret matches in my fringe-trimmed suede purse were for cigarettes. Which also never showed up in the shiny *Seventeen* world.

On the Dick Cavett Show, Norman Mailer called my idol, Mary McCarthy, a "trivial lady writer" and said her book *The Group* had "a communal odor that is a cross between MaGriffe and contraceptive jelly."

The pill was new. I went to college not sure if it was better to be a good girl or a wild girl. On the first Friday of my freshman year at the University of Iowa, I learned men spent the afternoon drinking beer at the Airliner bar, holding up cards to rate the women from 1-10 as they walked by. Nothing had prepared me for this. Now I was being measured against living, breathing women beside me on the sidewalk.

All these years later when I look at those pages I studied so voraciously, I can recall every impression each hairdo, each flourish of eyeliner made on me. I was thin, tallish, leggy and cute, with straight, shiny hair. Everything I was supposed to be in 1970. Yet, I never thought I was good enough. We didn't know about re-touching then.

41

We thought what was being presented to us was real. We knew we'd never achieve that perfection.

Have you seen the documentary *Miss Representation*? We were doomed from the start, ladies. Men—ad men, created the images they wanted us to conform to. It's worse now. Toddlers can call up porn on a handheld device as easily as they can roll around in the grass. This will not end well.

Beauty is still important to me. Now and then I click on articles about how to look younger, thinner, more chic. I'm not supposed to care anymore, at my age. But I wasn't taught not to care. I do look for beauty on the inside more often than not; and that's something.

I'm 60 now. I might get a cat, and name it Enid.

GIRLS WHO WEAR GLASSES
Robin Stratton

I'm 12 and I'm walking home from school, minding my own business, when I hear the familiar sound of boys barking at me and calling me a dog. As always, I keep my head low and don't look at them. Soon they'll get tired of it and stop.

But this time is different. This time they close in on me, and this time they're throwing rocks at me, shouting *Hey, Dog, where's your leash?*

I start to run.

I know I'm ugly. Do they think I don't know I'm ugly? Do they think I chose to be born almost blind in one eye, the eye that turns in, so that I have to wear thick glasses? And not just glasses—*bifocals.* Just the sound of the word makes me sick, makes me think of old, old ladies in a nursing home.

In every sitcom or movie about a girl going from ugly to beautiful, she starts out wearing glasses, then takes them off, and suddenly boys stop and stare. Whistle. Ask her out. Sometimes they are even too afraid to ask her out, she becomes *that* beautiful.

Take off your glasses, dates will insist years later when I am a grownup. *I want to see what you look like without them.*

I have never been able to see myself without glasses, but I know I must look better. Maybe pretty. So I don't want anyone to see me without glasses, because when I put them back on, I will be ugly again.

More years later, my boyfriend will pay $5,000 to have eye surgery that magically fixes my sight. After that first night of unbearable burning, of being terrified that my eyes are ruined, of having my boyfriend call the doctor to make sure that this agony is normal, I pull off the gauze bandages, and... I can see! I can see the clock on the wall, I can read the time! I can see my hands and... oh my God, I can read! I run into the bathroom, and there is my face, my beautiful face,

43

with no glasses!

But right now I'm 12 and I don't know any of this will happen. I don't know that one day I will not wear glasses and will be considered pretty. Because right now I am running from boys who are calling me names. The rocks don't hurt, but the words. Oh, the words.

BODY NOTES
Francesca Rendle-Short

50s

Are you ever too old to fall off a bike? Does it mean you should stop riding? It's true, you should have seen it coming: a wet day, distracted, riding fast on your Gazelle past Carlton Cemetery to get to an appointment, and you're running late; swerving to get around a person in the way, clipping a lip of bitumen…. Down you go. Books and notebooks everywhere. Bag and money rolling away. Your apple-a-day into the gutter. Ai Wei Wei lunch bag beyond reach.

There is something that quiets the spirit in the pause between a body falling down and getting up—strangely delicious.

You do a mental check—is everything alright? Did you curl your body on impact the way you learned to do it when you were young? People stop to bend over you. They wait to see you move. *Fuck, fuck, fuck,* you're saying loudly to anyone and everyone. It's not very dignified. Your body is in shock; nothing hurts just yet—you are alive. And then you feel the blood down your arm, all that is usually inside and contained beneath your skin begins to seep out. Splotches drip onto the bitumen. But it's a kind of miracle. Your body starts to heal the minute it is hurt. It knows what to do. Give it time and it will stop throbbing, scab up, start to get itchy, and peel—that's your favorite bit. You're not dead, yet.

You put together an inventory of votive offerings like the sort you see at the Wellcome Trust in London. Votive offerings: terracotta replicas of different parts of the body related to a promise, a vow—offered up as either blessings for what the part has given you, or as prayers to make better whatever the body part it is that's being offered. Here is a list of parts that are becoming more noticeable as you get older: skin, fingernails, eyesight, hearing, planter muscle, pubic hair, pelvic floor. Deliverance or gratitude, you're not sure which.

You write: "[G]iving weather to a newly found vocabulary, practicing call and response with an ear for sight-reading. Finding a missing body part, a hand, a foot, or a stray hair." (*Glossus*, 2013, 275)

Isn't it Marguerite Duras who talks about writing being naked, bare words in ink on the page? That writing is wild but that it also passes.

Someone on the tram offers you a seat and you decide to take it this time, why not, it's been a long day. Someone sneezes—bless you. Someone falls over on the footpath and breaks her ankle—a shopkeeper offers her a stool. Someone dies in the stalls while watching theatre and an ambulance comes—everyone goes quiet.

In Australia when you turn 50 you are given a present from the government, a Free Bowel Cancer Detection Kit. It arrives in a parcel unannounced in the post. Without ceremony, it tells you that you have shifted into a new bracket: you are now officially an 'old person'. In Australia, 80 people die of bowel cancer each week, and you don't want to be one of them.

You read the instructions on how to do the bowel test again: three easy steps, it says. You watch the YouTube video called "John in the John." You read: a sure sign of bowel cancer is blood in the stool or feces, rectal bleeding. The hardest part doing this test is to separate out doing a wee from a poo using your pelvic floor, which is out of condition, and the floating paper damn they provide you with, the Float Collection Sheet. Okay—poo there (you can't see any blood)—blue stick here with sample (red stick, second sample)—plastic collection tubes to slip it into—name the Collection Tube not the Transport

Tube—and a silver satchel to send it off to the pathologist at the right temperature. The instructions say you have to keep the sample between two and ten degrees Celsius (did you know Celsius is always written with a capital C). This free bowel test is more difficult than writing.

You still wear flowers in your hair, smelling good and looking like summer.

You are learning to sing again.

40s

Blood. You didn't know there could be so much blood in a single sitting—but there it is, the white porcelain of the toilet bowl has disappeared and now all the surfaces are red. The blood pours out as if you are a performance artist doing a reconstructed Buchamp, a feminist reinterpretation of *Fountain* that was refused exhibition at the Society of Independent Artists in New York in 1917. This toilet-work is wet—would it be censored today? It is dark red, a deep kind of black red, earthy tones but glossy too, shiny up from below, covering up the white surface from the pothole up to the oval ledge. There are clots in there too, darker and more sheeny than the rest, globules the size of fists. You stare at it, mesmerized. Impressed. Astonished. The red looks like it is moving, jiggling as a form of contemporary dance. Not reprimanding but smiling red as if on stage. All this from you? Is everything alright? Should you go and see someone? A doctor? An acupuncturist? Your mother? Should you ask one of your sisters—not that you could recall talking to any of them about menstruation—perhaps in passing, but not in detail, not to explain all this.

You write: "We hold mirrors to each other to ourselves. We forget to panic. (*But for air*, 2002, 1)

Nobody warns you of the change that occurs in your body when you start to stop bleeding.

47

Oh, I just had a hysterectomy and that really helped.
Oh, I've been through menopause; I didn't notice it.
You should see someone: that looks dangerous. Is everything alright?

You look up synonyms for womb: void, abyss, cavity, emptiness, interstice, nothingness, nullity, skip. You prefer the medical term, *uterus*, and technical details: inverted pear shaped organ located in the pelvic cavity of the female body of mammals; muscular; cervix and corpus. Your daughter gives you a plastic medical body for your latest birthday—she thought you'd be interested. You are. You pull out kidneys, stomach, big intestine, and little intestine in order to get to the bottom of the cavity, to get to that void, the uterus. To do it you have to take out the lungs and the heart. You wonder what it would be like to do anatomy in science, whether you should donate your body to science when you die.

You collect de-acquisitioned books from the library, dictionaries and anatomy books.

The Blood-Filling-The-Bowl-Red episode happens when you are visiting your father in the nursing home, crisscrossing Brisbane for supplies in the car. Your father has long retired; he has Alzheimer's; he needs help. So there you are in Herston near his old hospital—you have to stop somewhere, it's an emergency because two super-sized tampons and a pad won't fix it, and you don't want to spoil his car. You've got the medical school in your sights, the large expanse of green lawn and eucalyptus trees running up to the entrance, heavy wood openings onto the cool retreat of inside, brass handles on all the doors, wooden paneling along the corridors, white old-fashioned beveled tiles in the bathroom, pull-chain flushes from the ceilings, and those solid old-fashioned porcelain bowls.

You start to color your hair red. Fire-engine red. The less you bleed, the more red dye you use.

30s

Hair. When you think back to your 30s you remember hair, not blood, although blood is always there. Hair: hair marking out the different years. Soaped-up punk days, undercuts and hair extensions, peroxide and pink fairy floss reminding you of a wished-for childhood, bunches of pigtails and pony's caught up in scarves and clips. But not short like you think it should be if you're going to be authentic, Sapphic authentic. In any case, you don't think you are like them; you don't like dogs.

Then you fall in love with her and everything is windy and bright; the sun comes out. You see stars. There is no turning back. Really.

You write: *She is inviting herself to a feast... Loquat jelly lips. Sugary sweet and sticky.* (*Imago*, 1996, 5, 130)

20s

You bleed red onto fresh powder snow on the highest mountain in Australia and it looks like something has gone terribly wrong.

You fall off your bike slipstreaming through a cutting in a hill on your way out to university and the chemistry lab. You land on your chin and split it open. You are wearing your pink King Jee overalls and blood stains the bib. This is before you know about lesbians wearing dungarees as a classic staple (it is the 1980s), before you know you are one of them a decade later.

You write: "My throat quivers." (*Color of a seed*, 1998, 18)

And you have your babies. You don't realize then how much this will change you, your psyche, your thinking, your imagination (for the better), most of all your body; it will never be the same. Fine white stretch marks, nipples pointing downwards, dry skin, a thickened stomach like porridge. There is no returning to those pre-pregnancy more nubile days. No good returning to any pre-*writing* days either.

She is a yellow baby. Her bilirubin is up; she wears sunglasses to save her eyes. She has a full blood transfusion 24 hours after her birth, her small body in Velcro straps. She floats like an angel on white cotton clouds on the operating table as new blood drips into her veins. This looks like art only it's real. You cry yourself to sleep.

He is a blue baby. The umbilical cord is tight around his neck; there is not enough oxygen for his lungs. Birth is choking him. When they cut the cord, blood flicks uncontrolled around the delivery suite like water from a high-pressure hose.

You start writing in your journal, seriously.

10s
And you learn how to sing. This is where your voice comes from.

THE WEIGHT OF SILENCE
Heidi Stuber

140.8 lbs—Be careful not to go up.
I will learn to love this body. I will learn to love this skin. This is the year. I am capable of change.

Tangential avoidance is the best strategy. Stick to the periphery. No full-length mirrors. Look at your body only from the best angles. Work your way up.

Every day I walked two blocks to my best friend's house, catcalls echoing behind my ears: *whistle hoot hola chica smooch honk laugh.* I yelled. I flipped them off. I learned to curse in all the necessary languages. I wore baggier and baggier clothing to cover my prepubescent body. I crossed through backyards and took refuge behind freestanding garages. All the things I did.

How did your father respond? the Jamaican asks. *Did he go out there with a baseball bat? Did he walk you over every day?* I never told him, I reply. He stares blankly, speechless. In that moment, he decides he won't call again.

142.6 lbs—Acceptable. Barely.
Exposure therapy is the best strategy. Look in the mirror every day. Weigh yourself religiously. A number is not a menace. A curve is not a condemnation.

This is the part I would change, I say, this arc above the hips. I am precise, pointing out 3 inches in the bathroom mirror. *But that's where it gets awesome,* the Designer says, kissing the back of my neck, running his hands up and down.

In college, I took a self-defense class. A man in full-body padding like the Michelin man told us no one will help if you scream No! Better to scream out the names of specific targets as you fight back. Eyes! we scream. Nose! Groin! Who says groin, I joked. Much more fun to scream Balls in a cockney accent.

Strong is the new Skinny, the gym poster says.

145.4 lbs—Disgusting. Immediate action necessary. Cut all carbs and sugar.
I grew up wishing to be small. Small enough to slip through cracks in the pavement, hide behind bedposts. So small I disappeared from the landscape of girls with eyes leering back at them.

The body remembers. The body never forgets.

There are websites dedicated to the cause of wasting away. Hipbones that stick out like wings on a bird that can't fly. They say things like, *Inner Beauty is for Fatties* and *Pretty Girls Don't Eat.* Thinspiration, they call it.

Favorite Parts: Arms—Strong. Nose—Cute. Chin—Defined. Thighs—More when they don't touch. Calves—Buff. Muff— Awesome. Eyebrows—Thick. Hair—Like a lion's mane.

In 10th grade, my best friend who lived two blocks away weighed 88 pounds. Gain two pounds this week or I am strapping you to a hospital bed, her doctor threatened. We grew up lockstep: same size, same height, shared clothes. Today, she is a miniature version of me. In a photo of us on a mountaintop, she comes up to my earlobes, a doll woman. Too much, I think, too far.

35.75" Bust 28.5" Waist 36.75" Hips—Try to get to 28"

No. Stop. I don't like that. Quit it. Don't say that. Don't do that. You're being disrespectful. You're acting entitled. I'm done. Let it go. All the things I did not say.

The body harbors secrets. Shhhh. Don't ask. Listen. The body will tell you. The body won't forget.

We are lying in the Engineer's bed in the dark. What's wrong, I say, what's going on? It is the first time he can't finish and he turns away. Is it me? I ask. Am I too fat? There was only one right answer to this question.

Acceptable Parts: Feet. Cheeks. Mouth. Ears. Breasts—Could be larger. Ass—Men seem to like this part.

I kicked him out. I blocked his number. Don't ever call me again, I said. I deserve better. I insisted on more. I took a lover who looked at me like maybe I was magic. All the things I did not do.

36" Bust 29" Waist 37.5" Hips—Increase Bar Method to 4x per week.

My best friend now is larger than me. A size or two. We go to the spa together where she glides in and out of the water. Breasts buoyant, ass magnificent. A body not at war with pleasure. I could live in that body and be happy, I think.

Men have many words to couch their fear of fullness. Please be Petite, they say, Feminine. Athletic. No man in Seattle has the audacity to tell the truth. What they really want: Thin. Thinner. Thinnest.

Dedication to a cause is the best strategy. There are dietary changes, exercise routines. Try those first. You can always choose surgery later, if these remedies do not work.

Men like my body best in dresses. I like my body best when it is by itself.

Disgusting.
Shhhh. Listen to the remembering. Shadows—Nightgown—Panties—STOP. Wake up fully to the word pregnant. Feel breath freeze in the corners of your ribcage. Become small enough to inch backwards up your spine, away from the darkness, vertebrae by vertebrae. Disassociation, a therapist says, it is the body's way of protecting itself. The body is erasing what it can't forget.

Didn't he know? Ten year olds can't get pregnant.

Body Fat 24.6% - Try to get laid.
I bombard the Engineer with links about the pressure women are under. The insidious torture of the Never Enough. *I didn't know*, he says, *I never knew.*

But a feminist education cannot fix wanting.

Pilates. Pilates on an exercise ball. Running. Running Barefoot. Bar Method. Running Half Marathons. 32 push-ups for my 32nd birthday.

Yoga. Weight Training. Fancy Pilates on the MegaFormer©. All the things I did.

On my wall hangs the first piece of art I purchased. Typewriter print on a photo of a tiny room, a dark space: *Small places seemed safer.*

The body is trying to forget.

Body Fat 25.1% - Acceptable.
I find an old journal where I wrote a mantra to myself: *This is your body. This is the body God created for you.* How quaint, I think. I believed in God. Before.

54

I told them everything. I went to the Police. I wrote to the Mayor. I learned Karate. I remembered license plates of the cars that followed me home. I did not hide in a neighbor's back yard. I reported the man in the car, beckoning towards me, too excited to speak. All the things I did not do.

The body remembers. The body doesn't forget.

Disgusting Parts: Stomach—Not flat, never flat. Hands—Stubby. Knees—Weak. Sides—Saddlebags, Nana said. Eyes—Men always being annoying commenting on those.

I feel I need to clarify. I am not fat. I have never been fat.

Body Fat 25.7% - Disgusting. No sugar. Watch alcohol intake.
My body is a place. It is a place I am residing. I will learn to love this body. I am capable of change.

Disassociation is a convenient trick. Useful with lovers known and unknown. You're not usually so quiet, they say. What are you hiding? *Come back,* the Engineer says, *not like this.* Come Back. That passed for love, for me, back then.

Size 6 if I'm lucky. In designer clothes, size 10. Medium at most stores, small if the store is cheap. Size 28 jeans, except for expensive brands when I'm a 29. Size 8 dresses, to accommodate shoulders and chest, size 6 pants.

Your body is rocking, the DJ says, lying in my coral colored bed. Must not gain weight, I think.

1 out of 3 by age 16.
I pulled down my nightgown. I screamed. I pushed him away. I told my mom. He got the help he needed. I went to family gatherings

without cringing. My body does not carry nightmares. All the things I did not do.

The darkness lives on in my stomach. It is the worst part. The very worst part.

I look up the cost of liposuction, dreaming about flat surfaces, clean slates. I need double-paned windows, a new car, should be saving for a roof. But it is the recovery that deters me. There would be no man to take care of me, after I cut my body down to a forgetful size.

Skin. Muscles. Nerves. Secrets embedded in scar tissue. Breath frozen into bone.

Holding on to remembering is the best strategy. Draw your body out of the shadows. Stop trying to forget. This is the year. You are capable of change.

THE SCARS THAT MAKE ME
Jayme Beddingfield

I fell in love with tattoos at age seven. A green and black snake wrapped around a man's arm, one my mother kept hidden. I stayed quiet as they laughed and thought about which tattoo I'd get first. Tattoos are the scars we can choose—symbols of what we lose and fight for and believe. I saw that then, pain for art.

My mother only let me wear dresses. She never taught me to cross my ankles. *Use your beauty, you won't have it forever.* I sat in a school church pew between two boys, my ten to their fourteen. Both took turns lifting up my dress. When I went to the principal he told me, "Boys will be boys." A fire ignited in me. I would help see to it that those were words to stop saying.

They see me coming a mile away. I look like an easy target. I'm short and petite and pretty. I'm who they wait for in the parking lot shadows. Something written on my face says, "Fuck with me, put a gun to my head, I won't fight it."

Tears won't stop coming. I'm twelve, and for the life of me I can't figure out what went wrong. I try to explain, but the words stumble out in fragments that cut my throat. Before I can piece them together my dad asks, "Were you wearing that little blue shirt?" The memory haunts me even now, across the years and worlds between us. Having one's back is a two-person dance.

I hold an empty prescription bottle in each hand, both mine, both prescribed at my mother's urgency. She is still, deadly still, on the floor by my feet. That's why my mother had me lie to the doctor. I stow them away ashamed. If she won't fight, I will.

My mother always told me, "Your problems are your dragons. Defeat them. Rise above the dragons." I tried my hardest to figure how. It took years to see. She was my dragon.

I have my mother's glare. She's there when I'm angry or defeated, waiting with words about me and my body and all we've done wrong. "If you got it flaunt it," she'd say, pushing a black dress my way. No one used to see me. I was pieces of what was projected. Steal my purse. Push me against a wall. Tell me I'm no good. Take what you want.

Fingers in my throat, bent over the toilet. Mother's words circle in my head. Escaping the stress with control made it feel good. So good. I only left the house in loose clothes and a hat. If I had the power to turn invisible, I would have. Everyone said I looked good. They couldn't see I was sick.

One thing I know for certain, lost kids seem to find each other. We can smell it on each other. It's the familiar fragments that draw us near. I found broken boys and a new fascination. Lip rings. Studs all the way up the ears. The septum, the labret, the eyebrow, I got them all in a mall parking lot. Scars I still have, but these I chose. I'd get them all again.

My feet twitched, ready to flee. Some died, some were done talking to me. Everything was crumbling, an event I sensed coming. I saw the path that swallowed my mom a limb at a time. I was on it, but I was young. I looked across the county and saw hope.

So, I went with 3,000 miles of road ahead. I rode shotgun beside my best friend and our cat in my lap. A black dragon freshly inked in my skin hugged my left ankle, the first of many.

I was never a kid, and became a grownup before I was ready. Stumbling became a dance I grew proud of. I was doing it, breaking the cycle. All communications stopped. The 3,000 miles between us created mountains planes couldn't pass.

Stark metal. White walls. Masked doctors hurry. Concern harshens their movements. A gutting yank vibrated in my throat. I couldn't feel anything below. At first there was silence. I looked at my husband, my best friend, my love. We held our breath, and then we heard her. A primal, innocent cry painted a new version of us. I was never more terrified and altered than I was in that moment. I saw the point of all that happened. It was my turn to guide. A long scar below my bellybutton marked the day I became a mother, a second one soon to follow.

Now, my house is warm. The lights dimmed. My husband and I take turns saying goodnight to our two children, songs and kind words tucked in with kisses. I am good. We are strong. I am, and will fight to keep this. Birds and storybook characters mark my body, short and child-worn. My mind heals and grows and learns. I accept my imperfections and my scars, both the ones I chose and ones decided for me. I have a purple bird tattooed near my collarbone for the souls gone too soon. Alice in Wonderland falling down my forearm for inspiration and for the innocence I lost. The whale is for following dreams and for Ishmael, the first fictional character to whom I related. The bottle as a reminder I'm not my mother. And, there's a hobbit hole in the sky covering my shoulder that marks my heaven.

HOW YOU CAME TO LOVE ME
Monique Antonette Lewis

I saw a dark-skinned woman with big, kinky hair on TV today. She is everywhere now—in movies, car commercials, and fashion magazine spreads. I wish she was with you thirty years ago, when you were a little girl sitting on the floor between your mother's knees. I am full, thick and confusing and you believe I need to be straightened out. You relax me at nine years old. Every six weeks you repeat the process and I pray to God I don't burn. Part. Lather. Smooth. Rinse. Dry. Press. It is a time-consuming, often painful, sacrifice and I transform.

You run your fingers through me seamlessly. I look like the dolls in your closet. I look like the girls on TV. I look like the girls at school and you smile to yourself.

But I am not easy to tame. You mark the calendar for touch-ups so your mother won't forget to save me from breaking. I begin to tear in half. You cry when I clump and slip down the drain. You cry picking my pieces from the brush. You count my loose ends on the bathroom floor.

As a teenager, we develop a love-hate relationship. You are sick of the sacrifices. Sick of sitting in the priestess' chair. Sick of praying to God that I don't burn. And you forget all this when I am transformed like the women all around you. This is beautiful.

This is all you know until India Arie, Amel Larrieux, Lauryn Hill and Erykah Badu. They look like my old self: thick, kinky, tightly coiled and big. Aren't *they* beautiful? You cannot deny this. Others notice it too.

You want to set me free but some say I am unwelcome in a white man's world.

The priestess says you would have to cut me into a million little pieces. "You're not ready for that," she says and proceeds to part, lather, smooth, rinse, dry and heat.

New York, 2011. Women have taken back their God-given creation. Afros, dreadlocks, two-strand twists, twist-outs and bantu knots. Men and women compliment them in the streets. You have missed me all your life.

A new priestess has emerged. She takes your hand in hers and prepares me for cleansing. She understands my nature and you trust her when she thrusts the spear and I am born again.

* * *

There is beauty from the ashes. I am two days old but we have never felt so free. Gone are the days of burning and crying. Weeks, months and years pass before I grow full again and you understand my nature. I will never hang straight. I will have rough and smooth days. I stick out on both sides. I am going to knot at the ends and that is okay.

You love me for me. You say to me, *I am beautiful.*

THIGH GAP (OR LACK THEREOF)

Eloísa Pérez-Lozano

When I was growing up, my mom told me I was beautiful. She taught me to always be proud of who I am and to not care what others say. Even so, some parts of me were a little easier to love. I appreciated my well-endowed chest despite my superficial issue with natural asymmetry and blouse sizing conundrums. I didn't mind my narrow waist that made me look smaller than I was. Those negative couple of inches got me closer to the supposedly ideal hourglass figure assigned to the stereotypical Latina woman, which of course, I quickly claimed since I had no discernible Spanish accent or golden brown skin to announce me as such to the world. I liked my neck and the curve of my nape, how its length allowed for clinking colors to frame my face and dangle freely from my ears. I even accepted my square forehead that visually declared me my father's daughter, no matter how many times my mom wished it away during her pregnancy. But the one part of my body I could never embrace was my thighs. They always seemed like too much meat on my bones, and I'm pretty sure I haven't had a thigh gap since I was five.

In school, I hated wearing gym shorts because they would always ride up when I ran, nylon curtains eager to reveal my pillars of bone and flesh to the world. Because getting enough breath in me to avoid passing out was a higher priority than pulling my shorts down every ten seconds, the insides of my legs were always rubbing against, and at times pinching, each other. Like two siblings incessantly annoying each other on a really long road trip, but without a parent to stop them.

Eventually, that area of skin grew permanently darker from all the friction, a self-made tattoo marking my overly generous genetics. Only in bike shorts could I feel comfortable knowing that the fabric would suffer instead of my skin, fraying and subsequent holes no longer a shock after a couple of months. My thighs were always extra jiggly on the inside too, thick and juicy Jell-O shimmying with every step, and always a prime target for my mom's surprise mordidas de burro. If you're Mexican, you know these all too well: terrible stinging whole-handed pinches of white-hot pain on the inner thigh that make you curl into yourself, much like the hands digging into your skin. It's a maneuver she's perfected over the years, but luckily for us, she usually saved them for special occasions when we were all being extra rowdy so everyone got a taste.

Also, it's especially frustrating to cross my legs while wearing a skirt or a dress: First, I must open them quickly to unstick my thighs, (which of course, is not the most lady-like gesture) and then cross them carefully to avoid pinching. At least my leg muscles and fat are contained when I'm wearing pants so no maneuver is necessary there. It's the situation when I most wish I had less of them to deal with, when I daydream of how much less of a hassle it would be to have lean and slender stalks. For now, I can count on the fact that women with thighs like mine will always be Photoshopped in magazines, their leggy chasms digitally widened with a drag and a click.

Even so, I have come to appreciate the extra fat in interesting ways. When it's cold and I don't have gloves, I slide my hands in between my legs because no other place in my body can match that warmth. When rough-housing with my husband or family, I'm thankful for the strength they provide me, allowing for a leg lock to be that much more difficult to wriggle out of. On the occasion of a womanly emergency, I can count on them to join forces in holding back the Red Sea from invading the shores of my pants, at least until I can make it to a bathroom. And finally, after reveling in some delicious sex, the thick gates close and hold the slippery-ness inside, off the sheets and carpet long enough for me to reach the shower. Then they open and gravity takes over, pulling the clear after-course down to the floor of the tub before it makes a final trip down the drain.

I think of them as chubby little twins who are attached at the hip, one never wanting to be too far from the other, their identities melded into one. Twins who chafe and sweat as they work together to guard my most intimate openings, only drawing back when I decide it's time.

SENSITIVITY TO LIGHT

Molly Pennington

My first real headache entered like a train, sudden and mighty. I spent the night in a hospital. Endured tests and injections, but nothing could tear it from the tracks. Pain ran through my brain for months before it finally slowed. And since, for a decade, I take care not to rouse that engine.

I am a *migraineur*, which means prone to bad headaches and sensitive to sound and light. This also means I cover my face with black sunglasses and wear a huge sunhat even when it isn't sunny. Overcast days feel just as bright as clear ones. Gray sky is fluorescent and blinding. Snow is a giant, unrelenting flash.

My four-year old daughter knows that she may never scream. Because one shrill yell cracks my brain with lightening. And may not recede for days.

Screams sprout gardens. Red bulges. Thorns. This is why I huddle at the edge of children's birthday parties. Mistaken for the un-friendliest mother on earth. Really I'm just a hostage.

In the morning, by the first crack of eye, I can tell if I am in danger. If it feels like my eyes aren't eyes, but dangling yokes—if my brain isn't brain, but a bowling ball in an eggshell. Then I know. Today could bring a big one.

It takes about five hours, but a narcotic will dull a big one. I had to beg without seeming to beg. Step therapy had to fail. Still, doctors don't really get it. I can't say the pain is a ten. I mean, a ten is when I pass out or long for a bullet. When I really want to die, right? Was it a ten when I pushed out the babies? They both felt like burning trees stuck inside me from toes to torso. But I survived. Is that a ten? I can gash the head of the pain chart model with deep Bic striations, and still, doctors look at me as if I may turn to addict when I ask for

65

something to stop the pain.

"Perhaps it's just stress?"

Yes, my sensitive emotions. No.

Before they prescribed the mild opiate, they gave me depression aids. Some enhanced the pain. Made my "sensitivity" a stereo knob with a quick, smooth turn to the brake where the speakers blow. They didn't want to hand over a narcotic easy. I don't take it until "I can't take it," because there are consequences: the end of reason, a long dead sleep, a blank day or two after.

I need my days, each of them, because they form my life. I have seen and read the articles. The sexism about women's pain is like the pain itself, an affront, and hidden. I am calm and nice when I describe it.

Even during childbirth when the nurse's voice was way too loud and when she wouldn't stop talking, I didn't yell at her to shut up. My second son arrived the night the Midwife Center threw their annual donor party. I had to deliver in a small room in the back, the thunder of wine drinkers just over my head. Later, the center's director visited. I lay in the aftermath, bloody as a crime scene—one with a sleeping newborn.

"Thank you for being so good-natured," she said. Earlier I had longed for death, and then a caesarean. My screams felt animal. Like they came from a part of me that was not a part of me. After, I wept, not because he was born, but because it was over.

Was that even a ten? How would I rate the headaches?

The headaches that still attend me. The key, the dance of my days, is to make sure they don't enlarge. When they do I stake an outpost in my bedroom's doorframe and lean over a bucket in case I vomit. I like to press my skull against wood, as if I'm pushing back against that fist inside. My brain clobbers itself. Brass knuckles knead. Then they switch abrupt, to rolling needles. Another shift and fingers pinch the backs of eyeballs, yanking them rearwards while they expand. And if I move or think or speak, a crescendo of anguish floods me at once.

I shake and weep.

I cling to cognition even as I watch it go. Prayer, for instance, proves impossible.

It exists as some calculus far beyond my station.

"Pray for me," I murmur to my husband, though faith is dead and grief for it adds measure to suffering. Without God, I turn to people.

"What do people do? Tell me what to do? What do people do?" I am muttering.

The last bad one was a bad one because I had not yet been prescribed the thing that can stanch it.

Real godforsaken pain is so normal actually. So simple.

Through the stabbing-thinking there was this: thousands… or is it millions, currently suffer. Under torture. In hospitals. Childbirth. Other headaches.

"What do they do" I murmured again. "Tell me what to do."

If they are bearing it… how?

From experience, I know an ER is not the answer, even if I could get through the commotion of waking and dressing children. Dressing myself. Shoes. Seatbelts. Then drive through piercing streetlights toward just the word of some doctor: "migraine." Then a shot that doesn't help. It hasn't in the past on lesser headaches.

Finally, my husband consults the Internet. He puts my feet and hands in a basin of scalding water. Places an ice pack on my neck. Overcome with dizziness, I pass out into the numb cloud of mercy.

THE FAT FILLY

Wynn Chapman

It's hard to tell how many doctors my mother took me to before I started to think she was looking for something wrong. She had taken diethylstilbesterol (DES) when she was pregnant with me in one of the last years before they realized it caused deformities, hormone issues, and cancer in the offspring of women who took it. As a result, my body staggered into a particularly unattractive puberty, filled with "excessive" and "abnormal" everything.

The doctors' appointments kept coming. My mother picked me up early from school for blood draws or follow-up appointments. Sometimes I'd get to sit in the room with my mother and the doctor as he read the results: *normal* was the only word I understood.

Sometimes my mother would say to the doctor: "Can we talk privately?" and I'd be left in a hospital gown, bare legs dangling over the observation table as the two of them withdrew to his diploma-wreathed office. She came out looking sour and dissatisfied, we would leave, and I wouldn't see that doctor again.

I was a tiny child—bird-boned, pale, white-blonde -- and very nearly underweight. A man could close his entire hand around my wrist and easily make a fist. But as puberty set in, I began to put on slabs of muscle like a gymnast: calves like inverted bowling pins and thick thighs. I excelled at the butterfly on the swim team, my waist thinning as my shoulders widened. I was short and stocky and preferred short hair so that it wasn't hard to manage after swimming. Strangers started to confuse me as a boy.

"You were supposed to be so small," my mother lamented one day in the kitchen. "That's what the doctors said—that you'd always be pretty and thin."

The only thing that was true of those doctors' predictions was that while she and my sister made it to 5'8" and 5'9, respectively, I topped out at just barely 5'4". So her little white pixie had somehow become short and stocky and far too strong for a girl.

The light bulb went on for me at the last of the visits with the mysterious parade of blood-drawing doctors. This one was friendlier than the others. We spent more time talking without my mother there, and I made him laugh. He even let me keep my clothes on at the follow-up appointment for the blood tests' results, for which I was grateful and relieved. My mother sat there as he read off another litany of medical things, the word *normal* coming up again and again. Every time he said it, my mother shifted in her seat.

"Is there some other test you can give her?" she asked finally. I looked away.

"Maybe it would be helpful if you told me what you were looking for," The doctor said.

"I just think—" she lowered her voice as if someone in the hallway might overhear, "I think she has too many, I don't know, *male hormones* or something."

I could feel my face turning red.

"Mrs. Chapman," the doctor said, "There's nothing wrong with your daughter. She's *fine*, okay?"

They glared at each other.

Oh. It sunk into me. *She thinks I'm one of those "gays."*

I was, of course, though I didn't really know it then. And no doctor in the world was going to give her a Magic Pill to take that away.

***

I'd first felt that sinking on July 6, 1975.

For weeks my mother and I had been looking forward to watching the match race between Ruffian, the so-called *Fat Filly*, and Foolish Pleasure, the winner of the Kentucky Derby that year. "The Girl versus The Boy!" the evening news blared. There were buttons for sale at the grocery store of the mare's distinctive profile, and a general buzz of pure anticipation filling our shabby but clean rented apartment where my mother perched on the couch and I sat cross-legged on the floor inches from the screen.

Then there was Ruffian on the television, and she was winning. There she was with that remarkable stride until, a length ahead, both bones in her right foreleg gave out with a snap. There was the jockey, Jacinto Vasquez, doing everything he could to pull her up, to stop the catastrophe that was happening in her leg, the skin torn open now and blood spattering, ligaments snapping and the hoof flopping against the ground as she ran. She couldn't let herself lose. She tried to finish the race.

I was six years old. There were 50,000 people in the stands, a roaring sea of them, and 20 million people watching on TV. My mother was on the couch behind me and I was sitting Indian-style close to the television, so close that when I remember this moment: the sudden lurching of her gait, the jockey jolting upright in the irons and pulling the short reins back and back and my mother gasping *Oh my God* and the announcer shouting *Ruffian has broken down* again and again. I can still feel my eyes widening in terror.

My mother cried and I cried. We bought the commemorative magazines and watched the memorial shows and the Special Reports. We listened to the eleventh-hour calls for horseracing reform to protect the animals from this ever happening again, though it had been happening every day and everywhere and this time we all just happened to be looking when it did.

***

My mother never forgot it. She had a soft spot for animals that she never managed for children. She'd raised cows for 4-H, said they were "like big dogs," so she never ate beef. They came to her along the fence's edge as she walked up the dirt drive from school, calling to them by name. Her father once butchered one while she was at school, and when they sat down to dinner that evening, he took great delight in telling her she was eating it. I think there was something about animals that reminded my mother of some *good* part of her poor farm upbringing. I think this was why, besides cows, she had a particular affinity for horses. Add to this some strange certainty she'd picked up that owning a horse—any horse, not just an eventer or polo pony or thoroughbred—was seen as a sign of wealth, and we all soon found ourselves at a sad livestock auctioneer a few counties away.

The auctioneer was a huge, white-bearded man who wore a cowboy hat and spoke with the air of a ringmaster, some Emperor of Nags who showed off the cock-heeled, drowsy horses like used cars. A rap of his gavel and we were the proud owners of a stout brown and white horse that we boarded in a run-down stable outside of town. A second horse soon followed, though I can't recall whether it was the bay or the buckskin. Or was it Lady, the huge black horse that reared back and landed on my stepfather as I stood behind a tree at the paddock's edge? It could have been Aspen, the one with the pituitary problem who never grew beyond a yearling's size. Maybe Amigo, the donne? Cinnamon, the Morgan, or the Liberty, the tallish gray?

There were so many of them by the end. Most went lame, or we were told they soon would when the farrier came. We just loaded them, one after another, into the stable owner's trailer and returned them to the auctioneer. When we brought our hobbled creatures back, he *tsked* and apologized, told my parents there was *a bad one in every batch,* and offered them another for trade.

For a while, getting a new horse every few months was a thrill, like Christmas coming five times a year. But then I started to get attached to them, to wonder what the auctioneer would do with them after the stable hands led them away. I started wonder if it was right to go back to these pens of ragged horses over and over again.

The truth was my mother and I had different ideas about things even then. Like the way she thought the way things were on television was the way things should be, the *only* way. We should all talk like newscasters with no Southern accent, she'd say, cook the convenient ready-made meals from all those commercials, and look just like the people on the sitcoms and in the celebrity magazines she loved so

71

much. She wanted *normal*, one of her favorite words, a *normal* life that would play like a sitcom without the laugh track: the buffoonish Husband who earned well, the Good Dog, the beautiful Children, and the Horses chewing hay, their names affixed to their leather halters on shiny brass plaques.

We felt differently about a lot of things, like all those horses. After a while, I started to realize how *unattached* she was to them. At first she'd fawn on them, show them off to everyone at the ramshackle stable. But later, as we drove to the barn, I would hear the indifference. Everything became *wrong* with them, and they were gone soon after that.

The constant unveiling of "the new horse" to the other people at the stable was also starting to become strange. It evolved into a joke around the barn, but there was something darker humming underneath. The parade of new horses was starting to make them all uneasy, these people who somehow managed, I noticed, to keep same horses year after year.

One Christmas, one of the women gifted everyone in the barn with painted clay Christmas tree ornaments that were made to look like their horses, with careful attention to the correct sizes and colors of their bodies and manes. Each horse's name was hand-stenciled across its side.

We had a horse then, but the one she gave my mother didn't look like it. Instead, ours was painted like a patchwork quilt, and there was a question mark where the name should have been.

***

After the "hormone doctors," as they all became known, made it clear there was no medicine for what *what ailed* me, my mother turned to honing what would become her most potent weapon: shame.

The muscle I tended to put on could be controlled with less exercise and less to eat, with *more flattering clothes*, with nail polish and perms at salons with names like *The Look* and *Coco & Buff*. She took me clothes shopping and asked me to pick out things I liked, usually jeans or sweaters or button-up shirts in earth tones, white, or black. These were discarded and I was offered rough approximations of what I'd chosen in brighter colors, cropped lengths, skirts, and more *feminine* cuts.

"You're going to be losing weight soon so I'm going to buy this in a smaller size," she'd say once I'd finally agreed to one or two of them. She'd say this in front of the saleswomen behind the counter, giving them a knowing look and inviting them to chime in. They would turn to me with their Vaseline smiles and beam.

"*Good for you* for losing weight!" one would inevitably say, and I'd take the bag and hope the earth opened up and consumed me.

My closet filled up with garish, girly clothes in their various sizes, always at least one size smaller than the one I was actually in. I wore a uniform to school that had to be purchased in the correct size, so I didn't notice my scant wardrobe too much. I'd started to avoid going out much anyway. Years later the price tags still hung off their arms and legs like toe tags in a morgue.

My mother found a willing partner in her campaign when I was 12 or 13. Dr. E., General Practitioner, was a mannish woman who would stand in front of me where I sat on the edge of the examination table and tell me, over and over, that I was *overweight*. Vowing that it was time *to work on me*, my mother started taking me to biweekly weigh-ins with her new accomplice.

"You know we're finding people having heart attacks when they're 30 because they weighed what you weigh now," Dr. E. said once in her thick Spanish accent, trying to add *fear of death* to scare me thin and straight.

"You probably think you look fine the way you do," Dr. E. tried another day as I stepped off the scale. "But I'm here to tell you that you don't. What are you eating so much of anyway?"

"I like cereal," I offered softly. My face was burning red again.

"Well, this isn't just cereal."

Finally, she reduced me to tears. She asked me why I was crying and I just shook my head and looked away, wiping my eyes with the sleeve of my shirt.

"Just get dressed," she huffed and went out to get my mother. A minute later they disappeared into the office together, leaving me there.

"Well, thank you very much," my mother hissed on the car ride home, slapping the turn signal hard as we neared the house." Now she thinks you need to see a *psychiatrist.*"

***

Racehorses are notoriously hard to retrain. I learned this the hard way when I started volunteering at an equine rescue center here in Kentucky. You could tell the racers out in the pastures from the regular horses because their spines were missing the usual curve, the vertebrae instead forming a high, straight line from the neck to their rear. They aren't used to other horses coming toward them so they do poorly in a public barn, often anxious and unpredictable from being poorly socialized. They were sometimes aggressive and notoriously difficult for anyone but a professional to ride.

Sometimes the ex-racers dropped off at the shelter were so mean-spirited from a life spent running that they had to be put down. Others would be dropped off still in their monogrammed blankets, leather halters sporting their racing names on custom brass plates -- *Mr. Lucky*, and *Atta Girl*.

"The one thing you need to know about taking care of horses," one of the other volunteers told me as she trained me, "is that they're herd animals." We were brushing out a group of newcomers, checking their hooves, giving them a "socialization check."

I blinked. "Which means…?"

"I mean if you spook 'em, they'll run before they do anything else," she said. "So don't be in the way."

Horses don't like to stand still—it's not what they're built for. Ones that can't equalize their body's weight on all four legs are prone to inflammation; sores on their hooves become fatal. So when a horse injures a leg, the rest required to heal it is nearly impossible. Often a horse confined in a stall will channel its instinct for movement into a nervous "tap-dancing" that aggravates the break. Add to this the incredible expense of treatment, and it's something few owners even consider undertaking. They just have the animal destroyed instead.

Once while I was working at the center, I watched the volunteer equine vet evaluating a gorgeous chestnut Thoroughbred, its forelegs still wrapped with bright red tape from the morning's race. The vet bent the horse's left front fetlock and leg; the horse's tossed its great head back, its irises rimmed with white crescents. His assistant then trotted the horse down the length of the barn so the vet could check its gate.

Two times, three. The vet crossed him arms, unmoving as he watched the horse's clearly hobbled gait.

"Nope," he said sadly, shaking his head, and the chestnut would be put down the next day.

I couldn't help but think of Ruffian. When she woke from her three-hour surgery, she started running again, right there on the ground where they'd laid her on her side. They tried to hold her down as her thrashing legs destroyed the stall's wooden walls, the cast on her foreleg shattering her elbow so badly that one of the vets said the bones looked like a sheet of ice that had been dropped on concrete. There was nothing else to do. They buried her at Belmont with her nose facing the Finishing Line.

I lead the racer back to his stall knowing what was coming in the morning: the barren side pasture where they put the horses down, the starlings that would startle up in a dark cloud from the sound of the single shot. But even that dull grief wasn't enough to stop me from coming back to the stable.

That was another day, the morning I got to the stable before dawn, the two barn cats huddled atop the water heater near where the donated halters and blankets hung suspended on their hooks. We'd had new arrivals the night before and I went down the rows to see which horses needed brushing or their hooves picked. Outside one stall, someone had taped a sign: *Blind.* I went in.

The horse was standing with her head facing the corner, a smallish, pied brown and white horse with a wild blaze down the middle of her face. I murmured to her (*hey girl, hey*), her flank jumping as I laid my hand on her rump. I moved slowly, running my hand up her side as I neared her face. She turned her head toward the sound and her eyes, bluish white from the ghosts of cataracts, were uneasy as she sought me out.

When I touched her nose, she turned away from my hand and bumped the wall, jerking back. She bumped into me, startled again, and knocked into the wall. I shushed her until she went still, and then left the stall, something painful fluttering in my chest.

"There's a blind horse down there," I said to the barn manager in her freezing, cramped office at the stable's end.

"Yeah, I know," she said sadly. "Its companion horse died and the owners brought her in." She went back to writing entries in the feeding log book.

"'Companion horse?'"

"Yeah, blind horses have to be raised with a companion," she said. "It's like the other horse becomes its eyes. They spend all their time together like that."

"Can't we find her another horse who can be a companion?" I felt the panic rise in my chest.

She didn't look up from what she was doing. "No, they don't work like that."

I went back to the stall. Standing there, my hand on the horse's wide blaze, I started going through everyone I knew in my mind, picking out anybody who had a horse or owned some land. I wondered how much it would be for me to pay for the blind horse to be stabled here or somewhere else, imagined myself coming every day to care for her. I would talk to her until she knew me and wouldn't be afraid. She would come to the sound of my voice and I would walk her around the pastures and down the trails.

But I was in school then and could barely feed myself and my partner. And I didn't really know how to care for a healthy horse, much less one that had an issue like this.

There in the stall, the blind horse bumped against me again, pulling her face back. She blinked, sniffing me, and turned away. I finished my shift, brushing out the racers who'd taken a roll in the mud before last night's hard freeze, and when I walked out of the barn that afternoon, I never went back.

***

The Fat Filly is what they called Ruffian before they knew the remarkable horse she would be. She was big for a yearling and as comfortable to sit on as a sofa. She was undefeated in 10 career starts, and most of them she won in record time and by record lengths.

I knew all that, but what I remember most about her was how beautiful she was, how she bucked when she crossed the finish line and played all the way back to the stable after winning a race, how that lovely, dark head of hers was proudly on display on the wall of souvenir buttons for *The Great Match* in the grocery store that day. I remember the sound my mother made as the creature broke down under the strain, how Ruffian's ankle was left flapping on a bloody hinge. The chestnut racer in his blanket. The blind horse blinking and blinking and turning away.

I remember it all, and despite all my best efforts, some part of it has taken root and grown in me. I was supposed to be so small. I was supposed to be another person entirely, and when I look in the mirror now, I still look for her face. I will be 50 when winter comes again this year, and I fear nothing—not my mother gone or my wife's dear hands or the weight I still wear like armor—will ever take her away.

MISCARRIAGE

Bryne Lewis

"Miscarriage" was the first word I accepted from my body without any argument.

Even as a little girl, I had a sense of separation between my body and the life of my inner person. But when I was a girl, if we fought, we fought like sisters. Our competition for affection and approval was fierce, but knitted through by a ferocious love for one another. I always felt like my body was stronger and more beautiful than I had the courage to be. While my body demonstrated poise and dexterity, inside my head I cringed in fear of crashing a new drive of tumbles across the gymnastics mat. Along the ballet barre, no matter how smooth my movements in the mirror, I always saw myself the one snag in a row of identical, pink stitches. Physical perfection seemed as simple as good posture and a winning smile. If I hid behind that smile, then it was by mutual agreement and to protect my inner insecurities.

By the time I found myself wading through adolescence, my body had become the blank paper doll on which I wrote everything I thought would please an exacting (imaginary) audience. I penned volumes of celebratory newspaper clippings, award certificates stacked with accomplishment. But eventually, it began to feel like fiction. The combination of the pressure to present perfectly and the slick ease of pretending to be perfect added up to self-loathing. I felt marooned on an interior island. Soon, I began to starve. Actively. Rescue from my self-destruction did not arrive until college. Counseling helped some. Learning over time to listen again to my most basic physical needs helped more.

Even as I was relearning the edges on my person, like slipping into bed in the dark, a new mistrust developed. I began to experience stiffness in the morning, waking up with the physical memory of having wrestled a bear overnight. In the beginning, I pushed hard against my limitations. Fatigue and exhaustion at first felt like a victory. When I finally admitted that I needed help, the path to a diagnosis proved to be long and slippery with self-doubt. Doctors would shrug at my symptoms, preferring the credibility of their test results to my testimony. Drugs of increasing toxicity were the only help they seemed willing to offer. Soon, my illness and the side effects were competing to outdo one another in adverse effects. Once again, I felt lost at sea, my body a sinking ship. My only recourse was to learn how to swim, if not together, then in tandem. I changed my diet and exercise. I learned how to center myself behind closed eyelids to master the morning pain and panic. When I developed a second autoimmune disorder later on, I felt I could more effectively advocate for myself.

I was nearly forty and already mother to three older children when my partner and I decided to begin a family together. Although I had had no problems with previous pregnancies, I knew that this pregnancy could be difficult. But, most of my anxiety was about being able to conceive at all. After a full year of counting my life in 25 day increments, we finally saw the blue line in the little test window. I relaxed, reassured the worst was over.

And then I started bleeding.

Just a little. But amount of blood that is required to make a newly pregnant woman feel queasy is equal to what it takes a shark to show up in a nature show. I called my doctor. There was a conference about color; rusty brown was welcomed as a good sign. I was prescribed water and rest. And over the weekend, I medicated myself meticulously. Rest and drink. Drink and rest. With all the water, I was in the bathroom constantly, each time obsessively checking the tissue for trace amounts of blood.

On Monday, I felt crampy and uneasy at work. The pad I wore was a constant reminder that there was a reason I was wearing it, like a continuous car alarm in the parking lot that you just can't ignore. I went to the bathroom often and more than necessary. Things appeared to be okay. At least, I was no worse off than I was over the weekend.

Near the end of the day, on yet another trip to the bathroom, as I stood to hoist up my panties, there was blood suddenly everywhere. All over the tile floor. My panties and hose were unsalvageable and went into the garbage. Shaking on my hands and knees, I wiped up the blood like I was cleaning a crime scene. Somehow I got to my car without running into anyone. I fled.

From my car, I made the awkward phone call to my mom to tell her that I was 1) pregnant, but 2) needed to get to the hospital because I was bleeding. Together we spent the afternoon with waiting room televisions, stat blood tests, more rest and water, until we received the inevitable news that I was losing the pregnancy. My partner picked me up and we drove home together. I had never had a miscarriage before.

The first day is whited out with shock. There is a dim memory of hard cramping and then the very distinct feeling of tissue slipping through me.

The point at which I am able to bring the experience into focus, I am sitting on my back porch steps in jammie pants, coffee cup in hand. I remember numbly fumbling through facts: first trimester an unviable embryo almost always causes miscarriages. Forty and facing pregnancy, we had known ahead of time that we were playing genetic roulette. We had discussed contingencies if we were put in the terrible position of deciding whether or not we wanted to continue the pregnancy due to unviability.

On the back porch, I realized my body had made that decision, the right decision, for me. In the thick of grief, lemon-juice-on-paper-cut sharp, I relaxed into intense gratitude to my body for saving me from dealing with a much more difficult situation. For the first time in my life, I felt I could trust my body to make the right choice. My body was on my team. The rest of the miscarriage was a process of me agreeing with the process. With tears. With sadness that would blossom into depression in time for the winter holidays. I spent almost

6 months with my arms wound tightly around myself, gloriously not letting go.

When we did finally get successfully pregnant, I took the body confidence of my first miscarriage into my pregnancy. I rested like it was my job. I drank water with the best of them. I didn't argue with pain, hunger or fatigue. I listened and damn the commentary from anyone outside these bones, not in my skin. I held court from within my experience, insisting to doctors what's-what beyond their charts. Because I trust my body knows me best and we are better together. On that, we finally, thankfully agree.

HOW THE MANTAS HEAL

Dana Boyer

The white floodlights ahead of me are buried in the sand, sending up light that is turned blue by the deep ocean. It illuminates the plankton floating weightlessly in the currents, like the small shimmering dust particles on land that drift in any breeze. All around me the bubbles rise, columns of them, from my slow exhaling, from the regulators of the other divers, forming one translucent, shimmering circle. We have kneeled around these lights as if at an altar, our faces up towards the surface of this water, all eyes on the thirteen-foot manta rays that have started to gather.

They fly in, six of them, dark against the light's glow, their wingspan greater than most birds', greater than any of ours, their air this salty water, their dark toothless mouths gaping as they gather up the plankton made visible by our lights. They sweep past again, over top of us, in front of us, above the lights where the plankton thickly gather as a cloud, and back across, again and again.

This water, this deep black water where I kneel on the ocean floor thirty feet below the surface, is full of great miracles tonight, and these graceful, dark sea creatures are only one of them, because here I am, again, here is my body underwater again, and it is quiet, still, and in control. My lungs calmly breathe the condensed air that had to be taken with me in the heavy silver canister, and my hands grab confidently onto a rock to keep me from drifting away with currents that are caused by these circling rays.

Everything I have and am is now concentrated on this place, this underwater circle off the Big Island of Hawaii, in the middle of the Pacific. But a small part, one small corner, is vitally, achingly aware that my mind does not panic. I know the panic is there in my brain as if behind a fence, like a vicious, snapping dog through the small cracks, but for once, I have the strength to keep it there. I am clear enough to consider the mantas' beauty, and I am vividly aware that I had the strength to get here, because five years ago that would not have been the case.

I signed up for SCUBA diving six years ago because my husband craves difficult, extraordinary, and otherworldly things, and he was so excited that I became excited. And, like most of my life, I excelled at the classroom portion, I am most at home in the theoretical. But when it was time to hit the water, I panicked. My brain, slowed by a depression brought on by a hormonal imbalance that has occurred several times during my life, couldn't handle the strange fact of breathing underwater, it could not handle living in this different world where I did not belong. My mind could not comprehend the fact that I could survive in a place that was so clearly not meant for me. It could not cope with the idea that if I somehow lost my air, if my mouth piece popped out or if I forgot to check my instruments and I ran out, there would be nowhere else to turn.

I made it through my dive certification with plenty of hand-holding (literally) and some extra sessions with the instructor, dove a few more times, and then had two children and didn't do it again for five years.

Instead, for those five years my body did one difficult pregnancy followed by eleven months of severe postpartum depression, then another worse pregnancy followed by worse postpartum depression. I vomited up to twenty times a day and lost weight when I should have been gaining it for my baby, and then after I had him, I had lost all the strength I once had, mentally and physically.

A younger version of myself would have barely recognized the woman I had become. Weak in body and in mind, anxious to hand over hard tasks, shaken by any criticism, almost broken by any physical activity. Once a high school debater who now avoided arguments, once a softball pitcher who now had to lean on the checkout lanes in Target so I didn't collapse after a trip across the store. I turned down invitations to walk with friends, limited my outings out each day, and stopped doing all the things that I had loved doing most.

As we had taken the boat out earlier that day, that was the version of myself that was the nearest, and I shrunk from her and dreaded her. Like the difficult relative at a family dinner, I hoped she would stay away but feared that she wouldn't. On the way out, dolphins, silver and effortless, spun through the waves, through the boat's wake, through the surface of these blue Hawaiian waters. And when they fell away we looked ahead and saw something darker, something larger, the tail of a humpback splash and disappear, as if waving goodbye before leaving us behind for their deeper, shadowy world.

I watched these graceful creatures disappear while the instructors gave quick explanations for how we would follow them, using acronyms and names for equipment that I had not heard for years, the letters of the acronyms looking to me like they fell randomly from that clear Hawaiian sky. They were so foreign to me and I could no longer remember the context in which they went. The BCD, the regulator, the weights, how much weight I needed, which gear went on first, how to step off the boat. I knew I once knew these things, but I did not think the person I had become knew them anymore.

Now, under the water, my knees lightly on the sand, a tablespoon of water underneath my nose in my mask, something that had once made me panic so terribly I had ripped my whole mask off underwater, my hair floats freely in the current. My mind is at peace. A pillar of water in front and the manta rays above me. Flying, dancing, just missing us, never hitting each other in that small space, while the divers gather reverently around on our knees, buffeted occasionally by the surge created by such giant wings, but our eyes up, always up.

On the surface, in between the dives, the sun sets, and the city's coastline lights up, one light by one light, up and down the shore's edges and back into the mountains, as if candles are catching, orange and white glowing, while the sea horizon is too dark to see. And then we go down again, into a darker ocean, the blackness just beyond our flashlights, and my hands are steady, my breath does not catch.

My mind is clear, I did know how to step off a boat, I did know how to inflate the BCD. It turns out that the body does remember; not just the panic, but also the quick clearing of the ears so that the eardrums do not pop on the descent down to the ocean floor, it remembers the unstable landing on the sand, how easily the water can move me in this weightless world, and the way the currents hit the exposed parts of my face. I watch with amazement as my fingers do the quick diving signing motions that I thought I no longer knew. They communicate in this soundless world: yes, I am ok, yes, I still have air, yes, I will follow you, yes, I will be ok for a while longer now, yes I see that starfish over there.

It turns out that the body remembers both, the panic and the knowledge.

It turns out that the body does, in fact, keep a score, and that it is not always a negative one.

Twenty minutes in, fifteen hundred psi left, still gripping my rock and my knees occasionally bouncing on the sand, still mesmerized by this underwater dance that is so unlike anything I have ever seen or will ever see again, the biggest manta misjudges her distance. Or maybe she doesn't, maybe she means for this to happen, maybe she's curious or maybe it's for me, and she smacks me on the back of the head with her fin, hard enough to knock me sideways, hard enough to roll me over in the water. And I gasp from the surprise, from the pain, and from the fear that maybe that cracked the fence to let that growling, lunging panic through again. But I breathe, I readjust my snorkel, I clear my mask, and I turn to grin at my husband. The fence stays secure.

Sometimes, finding myself again, in body and in mind, means breathing compressed air through a rubber mouthpiece in a completely different world.

Sometimes finding my strength again means getting knocked down by a manta ray.

Sometimes my body's redemption can be found on the bottom of the ocean.

INTERSTITIAL CYSTITIS

Paula Bomer

On my son's first day of Kindergarten, I pissed blood. Freaked, I went to my midwife. It was a supposed urinary tract infection. My midwife gave me a prescription for antibiotics before the urine test came back. I took them. Later, it turned out, the test came back negative for a UTI. The pain got worse. I took over the counter drugs, which turned my piss blue. I went back on antibiotics. Peed in a cup. The test came back negative. This went on until one time, I ran into the midwives' crowded office, crying, bent over in pain, and demanded help. The head midwife, it was a group practice, came out and sternly told me I couldn't behave like this and I needed to see a gynecologist.

For the first time in eons, I went to gynecologist. She was amazing. I thereafter saw her regularly. She was horrified about the endless antibiotics. She let me cry. She took my pain seriously. She said I needed to see a urologist.

The first urologist I saw in the Clock Tower near my house was a middle-aged man with Viagra flyers all over the office. He gave me antibiotics. I have a memory of visiting my parents in Austria, and sitting next to my husband, swilling down antibiotics with a large bottle of beer. I remember this because I also remember feeling ashamed and hopeless.

Then, walking down Dean Street, a block from my house, I ran into a woman I knew from an old mothers' group that I was a part of, that imploded in the usual fashion of just too much bitch behavior, and she said, "Hi, how are you?" and she didn't really care how I was but I didn't care that she didn't care. I burst into a diatribe of all my bladder problems. Then she said, "My husband's sister is one of the only female urologists in NYC. You should go to her."

God bless that woman, an uptight middle-aged lawyer, who showed me so much kindness in that one moment. Funny how transformative even a moment of kindness can be.

I went to Bill's sister in the Upper East Side. She gave me a five-time supply of antibiotics. I took one course of it. And the pain worsened terribly. I went back. I was angry. I said, "It made the pain worse." She did something which involved putting a tube in me, and there I was, in a paper gown, naked, so vulnerable, so desperate for help, and when she took the tube it out it hurt, and I started to cry, and she said, "I'm sorry."

I said, "I always had a high tolerance for pain. When I was a little girl I broke my elbow in three places and didn't cry and no one figured it out for days until I finally turned green with pain and my mom took me to the doctor. And I gave birth twice with no drugs."

She said, "The thing about chronic pain is it makes you more sensitive to pain. It's as if your body can't take it anymore."

I said, "I think I have interstitial cystitis," because at that point I'd been on the Internet.

She told me to stay off the Internet. And then she said, "Go see these pelvic floor physical therapists," and gave me a prescription for it.

Did you know that bladder is a muscle? That it can shrink or grow, like any muscle? Did you know that Interstitial Cystitis is sort of like having ulcers in your bladder? Did you know some women who have it get their bladders removed, wear those bags to collect their urine, and *they still are in pain?*

At this point, my husband and I were barely talking. I loved him but hated how he treated me. So I also just hated him. At one point, sitting on the porch at our house upstate, he yelled at me, getting in my face, "You're sick and you do nothing about it. It's your fault and I'm sick of it."

This, after seeing a million doctors. I had a rare moment of calm, and I said, "You don't like it when I'm weak. And you should see a shrink. I can't always be strong for you. You're afraid." Or something like that.

The pelvic floor physical therapist was a bit life changing. The first time I saw her, I wept. I told her everything. Then I lay down and she put her hand inside me and massaged. Then she hooked me up to electrical stimulation. I felt a bit better. I saw her twice a week. Then once a week. I cried sometimes. I love that woman like you cannot know. I called the gynecologist and told her what was up. She was very interested. The gynecologist went out to lunch with my therapist's boss, because she was very interested in this sort of new field. At lunch she sat at a table next to Keanu Reeves and asked for his autograph. He was nice.

I also started seeing an acupuncturist who also did body massage. The first time I saw her, I sat across from her desk and I wept and told her everything. I've known her now for fifteen years. She gave me gentle herbs that helped. She needled me. She gave me amazing massages. I started to get better. I did a ton of yoga. I suffered and got better. Slowly, I got better. I gained weight. Slowly, not everything I ate burned my insides.

I was healed by women. Women who cared about my body. Women touching my body. Women listening to me cry, women healing me. I think I needed that, needed intense caring, needed women knowing me so intimately, touching me so intimately.

My husband saw a therapist. That fall, over thanksgiving break, we went to visit his family, staying at a house nearby. I curled into a ball on the bathroom floor, crying and crying, saying "Go without me." He did. Later, I did go to his family's house. That was the last time. That was twelve years ago. And since then, our love has blossomed. I feel safe, for the most part. Safe with him now.

This morning, I was making my endless jokes about how he should leave me for a young woman because I'm 46. He said, "I love you."

I said, "No you don't," and pulled the blanket over my face because he was coming over to me, dressed for work, a little late for work because I blew him and then we fucked.

And he kissed my face over the blanket, maybe three times. And he said, "I always loved you. I just wasn't very good at it."

MY CROOKED LITTLE SELF

Katharina Love

I spent my summer of 2012 horizontal on an old comfy couch in my best friend's basement apartment. I wanted to get up and join the fray, but I could not rouse myself from my prone position. This was not my normal state of affairs. Concerned, I dragged myself to my doctor to reluctantly address the elephant in the room. The elephant in question? John Merrick.

When I was a small child, my grandmother took me to see *The Elephant Man*, a movie about an Englishman with severe deformities. In the late 1800s, Merrick was exhibited as a human curiosity. The depiction of John Merrick terrified me for reasons other than the obvious. I was terrified of John Merrick, because I was John Merrick.

For as long as I can remember, my mother has told me that I am bad. What constitutes bad is still mysterious to me. Yet, I know not looking like everyone else has certainly played a central part. For my mother, it was paramount that she had a daughter who looked just right. A Kate Hudson to her Goldie Hawn. Instead she had me. Me, with my crooked smile and my speech impediment.

The '60's were not a time that embraced difference. The children at school echoed the verbal abuse I was experiencing at home. They called me names and laughed at me. I had no friends and would eat my lunch alone in the girl's washroom. I knew those kids at school saw me just as they saw John Merrick. An oddity. A freak. Something less than human.

I ran from my feelings. I ran from my truth. I ran for 45 years, until that moment in my doctor's office when I could run no more. I told him of my anxiety and my exhaustion. I confessed my self-hatred and persistent feelings of otherness.

My doctor first sent me to a geneticist who wondered if I might have Down syndrome. I did not. I was then shuffled off to a neurologist who noticed unusual movement in my eyes. He sent me to an opthoneurologist, who excitedly told me I did not have peripheral vision. I did not share in his excitement. In crept fear, and its friend anger was soon to follow. I was not Exhibit A-7349. I was Katharina Angelina Love!

I went to a second geneticist, who specialized in rare diseases. Finally, I was given the answer I had been so long searching for: Moebius Syndrome.

What in fresh hell was Moebius?

The geneticist explained that it is an extremely rare congenital disorder that affects primarily the sixth and seventh nerve. Dutifully, I took the booklet of information and looked through the photos. This was my worst nightmare. I focused on the frightening photos of men, women, and children who had serious facial anomalies. Is this really who I am? If so, then my mother was right. I am freak. I am bad. I am a bad freak.

All I ever wanted was to have a great big toothy grin, so I wouldn't have to witness that fleeting look that passed over most people's eyes when they first meet me. I abhorred that look. The look that both singled me out and dismissed me.

During my freshman year of university, I came up with a plan. I believed all my troubles would disappear, if I could somehow become beautiful. Then at long last, I would be deserving of love.

That was certainly the message I received from my image obsessed, social climbing parents. I was raised not to become a doctor or a lawyer. I was raised to become a doctor or lawyer's trophy wife. In order to get the title of Mrs. and that final rose, I had to become beautiful.

For their sake and mine, I went all in. I had rhinoplasty, a chin implant, and a breast reduction. I poured toxic chemicals on my hair turning my naturally brown locks into long blonde hair that even Farrah Fawcett would have envied. Women would come up to me on the street, telling me how much they loved my hair. Men began to ask me out on dates. The long-stemmed roses arrived, and the Dom Perignon flowed. The beautification of Katharina was complete. My work was done.

Except that it wasn't. I was keeping a secret. Something that made me feel on the inside as different as my former physical self on the outside. I was attracted to women. Exactly what was I to do with those feelings? I had finally found social acceptance and my family's conditional approval. I was unwilling to give up their love and admiration.

In graduate school, I dated many of the single Jewish men in Toronto. Ultimately, I found Robert, my future husband. I became pregnant and walked down the aisle in 1991. I now had a child, a home, and a husband. I should have felt happy, but instead I was feeling more and more discontent. If I was going to be a role model for my daughter, I needed to find and claim my authentic self.

I divorced Robert and slowly began the coming out process. I went back to school to study Psychosynthesis. I opened my own psychotherapy practice. All went swimmingly until the summer of 2012 when exhaustion took me over, forcing me to look deeper into the caverns of my psyche.

I needed to accept my differences and come to peace with my flawed and fractured self. I came to realize that only through self-acceptance can I find the love I so crave. This is the love I have been searching for all my life.

I have made the decision to spend the rest of my life seeing the beauty in, and making peace with, my broken crooked little self.

KEEPING TIME
Rachel Mans McKenny

Breasts aren't like a digital watch. They don't come with a pamphlet. Their purpose is fuzzy, but for women it's easy to keep time by breasts. At ten, my breasts were a hope with an optimistic purchase of a training bra, three years too early. At twenty, my breasts synched tight into corsets for theater performances. Power was a high mountain of breasts. Laced in I felt gorgeous and bosomy, and the two words were interchangeable. Now my breasts keep time, and there's no reset button.

After my mother had her mastectomy, the cuts under her armpits ran across her chest. She was as finely stitched as the quilts she knitted. Her hair a thin spool of thread. I missed the soft place between her arms, and the color in her cheeks. I missed my soft mother.

My mother had her mastectomy a few months before my wedding. While she underwent chemo, I took a week off of my final semester at graduate school to care for her. We'd play scrabble and I'd cook her tasty meals with the hope she'd taste again. *My mouth*, she'd tell me. *It all tastes like vinegar.*

She finished her chemo pills a few weeks before my wedding and in the pictures, the two of us squeezed our cheeks together, our matching freckles across the bridges of our nose. Her breasts were the size mine are now, 36B, but in that wedding picture there are no curves, no hills, or valleys. Her dress covered her stitched scars while my makeup covered my blemishes. We looked into the camera, eyes bright with matching hazel.

At present, my breasts are lap timers. They are workhorses. They've fed two crying babies on airplanes and comforted my once hungry infants in church pews. But they are an alarm waiting to go off.

When Angelina Jolie announced her decision to remove her breasts in a preemptive cancer strike, I read every news article that flooded my direction. She was the heroine in her own movie, and she was cutting the wires to a ticking time bomb.

But I don't know if I can cut the wires. I haven't even been tested for the BRCA gene, a gene linked with cancer, which Jolie inherited. My mother's cancer wasn't BRCA-related. With her diagnosis, though, I become a direct descendant of her cancer. I'm at the cusp of thirty, and getting ready for my first mammogram. It's a coin's flip: Heads or mastectomy? I'm not ready to let go of my breasts. I will miss them if they go.

When I hold them in front of the mirror, I imagine Barbie-like breasts, areola-less and reconstructed into small silicon mounds. I see thin scars against my chest. The scars look soft like my mother. They keep time more than I ever could.

HOT TEACHING

Lucy M. Logsdon

I'm lecturing on a reasonably mild day. My college's heating and cooling system seems, for once, to be in sync with the actual outside weather. Still, I've dressed in layers: black silk tank top, zazzy striped pullover sweater, long brown vest, and a very light tan jacket—this is October. Sudden changes can occur. My students are attentive, cell phones down, eyes focused. I could even say a few are almost perched on their seats. I love this lecture; it has a pattern. Start with having them define the general concept of poetry, then, via PowerPoint and hard copy books, widen the definition of what poetry might be. I'm almost to the key point. The shift: not only what might poetry be, but what might poetry do? And, then, boom, what has poetry done already? I've got political slides, I've got music videos, I've got protest poetry and news footage from past to present.

My lead-in has worked; I've gotten the rhythm, the pace right. I pause to drop the big question. And then it starts: the very first drops of sweat. The feeling of my face both flushing and blushing. Damn, it's hot in here. I peel off the upper layers. I can sense, hell, I can see the students shifting. Do I ask them if it is hot in here? They don't look hot. One female student has even wrapped a shawl around her shoulders. She looks cold. More sweat forms. This isn't like exercise sweat—somehow this sweat, this fluid is different. The liquid just oozes out, fast, so that I'm bathed in a full layer of wet.

I have to pull my zazzy sweater off to wipe the water, the whatever the fuck this is off my arms, and then my brow and face. I mean—what the hell is this? I'm obviously a) dying, b) having a heart attack, c) suffering from a full immune system collapse, d) experiencing the sudden emergence of a parasite I contracted years ago overseas, d) having a nervous breakdown, e) paying the price for all recreational drug use in one giant flashback, delayed (by a decade or two), f) all of the above. Now perspiration has dripped down onto my glasses. My fancy lenses are so blurred, I can't see a thing, but I can feel my face — particularly my cheeks and chest—reddening and splotching.

If I were to look in a mirror, I would see what appears to be an angry case of hives. Again, I have my students' absolute, utter, full attention. There are no non-traditionals in this section; they are all blissfully, stupidly, disgustingly young.

They are also concerned; I'm older than most of their parents (though they don't know that). But they do know—something is off. What is happening to Ms. L?

They pretend everything's fine; I pretend everything's fine. No bizarre, uncontrollable body things happening to your instructor up here. I will NOT ask "Is it hot in here?" I've totally lost the point of my lecture. Something poetry. Something politics. Where the fuck is the cool music video? I push frantically at my computer and SmartBoard. The speaker system won't work. It has always worked. I pull up YouTube—I will play anything right now, with or without sound.

I manage to punch in Woodstock. I manage to type in The Band. Levon, my savior, appears on the classroom SmartBoard screen. There's no sound, but there he is, and then, miraculously, I hit some key combo that returns the sound. Levon is in the middle of singing "The Weight." I use my black silk tank to wipe my glasses, so I can, at least, partially see. I have offered almost no explanation for the music video from Woodstock on the screen. I have not explained Woodstock. But, I have slowly started to turn a lighter shade of red.

My students are still stiffly acting as if nothing at all strange or bizarre has happened. Everything is fine. And, then, the group's harmonizing is so good on this take that my students start listening and forget about me, and forget about class, and forget about poetry. I open the door, step out into the hall where there's a water fountain one foot away. I splash and drink as much cool water as I can. I lighten up. I can feel the change; I've lost at least a pound or two in water

95

weight. Levon keeps on. And I push on through.

MIGHT AS WELL

Ali Beemsterboer

I put the piece of paper under my tongue, wait for it to dissolve, for my body to dissolve into the carpet, into the bed, into thin air. The paper gets soggy and stuck in my permanent retainer. As the LSD takes hold, the walls start to breathe, the fur on the cat becomes softer, colors become brighter, and my body becomes thinner. I examine the prickly hairs on my legs without a care that I'm not clean-shaven. I stretch out so my tummy feels flat, rub my hands over my suddenly silky stomach.

"I can feel my insides," I say, pressing on my abdomen. That's how thin I feel.

"That's not good," my partner says.

"I feel sexy," I say. This is not what I see when I am sober. When I am sober I see chunky, chubby, clunky. I see how, when I bend over, my ass bumps into things. I see my buh-thighs (a family term for the fat on the side of the thigh, little handles like a second set of ass cheeks).

And what I feel is pain, physical pain that reverberates through my body, an invisible disease, fibromyalgia (aka: "We don't really know why you hurt. There's nothing wrong with you.") Random little pin pricks, nerves acting out. Headaches that creep from the base of my neck and stuff themselves in the back of my head. So often it hurts to be touched on the legs or arms. I shy away from my partner's hands. And I can't help but wonder whether my perception of my body itself produces the pain.

But now, pupils dilated, perception warped, my body disappears— I don't feel it. I want it to stay this way forever. While my partner has difficulty moving, I move more. I dance, and touch myself, and lounge around naked. I say, "I love my body," and I melt into my partner's arms. We laugh when I cannot get his sweatpants over my ass.

And I am afraid, sad even. Sad that this drug will fade, that I will return to my fat and painful body. "I don't want this trip to end," I say. "I want to keep loving my body." I start to cry, every tear multiplied into a hundred by the LSD.

"I love your body," my partner says. But that will never be enough.

And it does happen. When I come down, it feels as though someone drove a stake through the back of my head and down my spine. I lie down, pressing the trigger points on my skull to help me fall asleep. I know I over-did it.

One thing psychedelics reveal to me is where I spend my conscious thought. So much of my consciousness, concerned about the size of my body, reading diet fads: *don't eat carbs, don't eat sugar, don't eat fat, don't eat.* So much time spent managing the pain: *how much sleep to get, when and what to eat, stay moving, but don't work too hard, try not to think about it, don't be negative.*

And yet, after the trip, I'm left wondering where else I might spend my conscious thought. The mind/body duality, an illusion produced by the human capacity for abstract thought. Mind cannot escape body. Even when I vacation on a tropical island in the comfort of my own bed, even on a psychedelic trip: I obsess over my body.

I might as well learn to love it.

DON'T GO NEAR THE WATER

Eve Fox

We run the short distance from the house to the pool, zig-zagging between the grass and the sidewalk in the bright sunshine. Everything here is incredibly neat, the cars—all newish—look like they've just come from the carwash, the small streets and cul-de-sacs are all freshly paved, and the grass looks groomed rather than mowed. It's like being dropped in *The Truman Show*—a far cry from the house my dad built for us in the pine-scented woods back home in Woodstock.

It's the summer before 5th grade and my best friend, Hannah, and I are spending a few days visiting her grandparents in their gated community on Long Island. I like Grandpa Morris—he's almost 80 but seems ageless. He still has most of his hair plus a quick, dry wit that makes me laugh. His humor is mostly lost on Grandma Judy who is sweet if rather tightly wound. She's always wiping down the already spotless countertops. But she's a great cook and I am a sucker for her sweet and sour meatballs and her Mandelbrot. Aside from mealtimes and a trip to the mall to buy us a few things, the grandparents leave us to our own devices, which is fine because we are in love with the swimming pool!

The woman at the little gatehouse outside the pool enclosure smiles, waving us inside and handing us big, fluffy towels. Grandchildren are a precious commodity here and we are treated like beloved pets by all of Morris and Judy's friends. It doesn't hurt that we are still cute—our skin unblemished, our noses proportionate, our armpits hairless, our breasts not yet budding. We don't talk about it but we're both quietly reveling in the novelty of being the stars of the show here, even though our audience is made up entirely of elderly Jewish people.

There are no spiteful older brothers around to steal the limelight and make us cry—just us and our adoring public.

We choose two lounge chairs, draping our towels over them and pulling off our shirts, shorts and sandals, leaving everything in a jumble on the concrete. The pool is massive, shaped like a T-shirt with the arms serving as shallow ends and the trunk providing a place for people to swim laps. Since we are not very tall and have no interest in vying for lane space with the few swim-cap clad residents who are in the pool at this hour, we stake our claim to one of the arms—no one minds—there are very few people around. We hold our noses and turn somersaults like mermaids then dive down to touch the bottom and stand on our hands with our ankles sticking up above the water. We flip our heads forward, then flip our hair up, letting it balloon out over our foreheads to make what we call a "Martha Washington" hairdo.

The sun is hot and the water is full of chlorine. I've left my white, wire-rimmed glasses on the chair next to my pile of clothes. When I come up, my vision is hazy even after I clear my eyes. I stick my finger in my ear to try to clear some of the water out and see that Hannah is standing by the edge of the pool talking with a very tan man who must be in his early twenties. She's chattering away in a high voice and I swim over to hear what she's saying.

The man looks like a lifeguard. In addition to his deep tan, he's wearing a Speedo and has short hair and a muscular build. His voice is deep. "What's your name?" he asks Hannah. She tells him. "And what's her name?" he asks, pointing to me a few feet away. "That's Eve," she says.

"Hi Eve," he says.

He asks some more questions, talking flirtatiously. Hannah answers him in a quick, high-pitched voice that makes her sound even younger than 10. Something's very wrong here. When he addresses me, I respond in leaden monosyllables. I do not want to talk to this man.

His comments get more and more familiar and he keeps moving closer. My heart is pounding and I have that feeling I get when my mom, who is not the best driver, has just narrowly avoided an accident—like something thick and hot is pumping through my veins.

100

It's as if I came up for air and spotted a dorsal fin cutting across the sparkling surface of the shallow end.

It's probably only been a couple of minutes but time has begun to behave strangely, stretching out in a nightmarish way. I finally force myself to swim away to the other side of the pool. I feel awful for leaving Hannah there but the need to get away is too strong to deny.

"What's wrong with Eve?" I hear him ask.

"I don't know," she says in that unnaturally high voice.

I climb up the ladder and head for the chairs, wrapping myself in one of the towels the nice lady gave us. After a moment, Hannah joins me. "Are you okay?" she asks.

"There's something wrong with him," I say to her, quietly, afraid he will hear. "Why does he want to talk to us? We're way too young— it doesn't make any sense."

"Maybe he's just being friendly," she says. Despite her parents' divorce and the fact that she's been to both Florida and California while my parents are still together and I have been exactly nowhere, Hannah is much more trusting and naïve than I am. Maybe it's because my older brother is much crueler than hers is. Maybe it's because I've been raised in an atmosphere of subtle paranoia—my dad lost his dad at 13 and he's always waiting for the other shoe to drop. Regardless, there's no way I can ignore the alarm bell that's tolling in my head and I do not feel compelled to "make nice" with this creep.

He comes over to our chairs, sitting down next to me, the curly, blond hairs on his legs glinting in the sun. He touches my leg casually and I freeze, "Are you going to come back in?" he asks.

"I don't feel like it," I say, looking down.

But Hannah agrees to join him. I'm flooded with guilt as she climbs down the ladder into the water but it seems I can only save myself.

I lie on my side, wrapped in the towel. I don't want any of my skin exposed. I close my eyes and pretend to sleep, every muscle tense. Hannah's high voice is chattering away in counterpoint to his deep rumbles though I can't make out what they're saying. Everything is a jumble. I am confused, frightened, embarrassed, defiant. Am I wrong?

101

Is he just a friendly guy with no one his own age to talk to? After all, everyone else here *is* over 70. Am I being rude? But shouldn't he be saving this kind of attention for some busty girl in a bikini who has at least gotten her period? I feel trapped on my little lounge chair island. I won't go back in the water but I can't leave without her.

A shower of drops lands on my face and I open my eyes. Hannah is standing over me, teeth chattering, eyes averted, water dripping off her purple one-piece bathing suit with the little red lady bugs all over it—my favorite.

"Let's go," she says with urgency. I grab my stuff and we retrace our path in reverse—all the innocent joy of the morning extinguished.

When we get back to her grandparents' house, I feel exhausted and dirty. I escape into the bathtub in the guest bathroom where I sit in the hot water, my heartbeat eventually slowing. What just happened? When I come out, Hannah is sitting on the bed in her bathing suit, wrapped up in the bedspread and looking as miserable as I feel.

"That guy in the pool really scared me," she says.

"Me, too," I say. She's clearly uncomfortable and I don't ask her what happened. I'm not sure I can handle anything more.

Later that afternoon, I develop a sore throat and a raging fever. Now my physical state matches my emotional state. I lay on the scratchy, polyester bedspread on one of the twin beds in the guestroom, watching the white fan spin, engulfed in misery. Hannah and I are very quiet—too overwhelmed and ashamed to talk about what happened. And there's no way in Hell we're going to tell Grandma and Grandpa about the shark in the pool.

When Hannah's mom arrives the next morning, she asks if we want to go for one last swim before we head back home. "NO!" we say in unison, surprising her with our vehemence. We say goodbye and thank you to Grandpa Morris and Grandma Judy, give them hugs and get in the car. The seats are covered with hair from Hannah's dog, Bear, who I love even though he drools all over the windows whenever he's in the car. I sleep most of the way there, tired out from my surprise sickness and from pretending nothing is wrong.

When we get home, life goes on as usual. My brother teases me mercilessly when he's not ignoring me or trying to conscript me into one of his elaborate games or home movie productions. I escape into books. I especially love Judy Blume's *Starring Sally J Friedman As Herself* and *Are You There God? It's Me, Margaret.* School starts again and Hannah and I are both in Mrs. Klotzberger's fifth grade class. At recess, Chinese jump rope, which we loved in fourth grade, has been supplanted by box ball. I love standing in the box and smacking the ball across the yellow line as hard as I can. We girls are rather vicious when we play. It feels good.

Later in the year, my breasts do begin to grow, much to my dismay. Hannah remains flat as a board for many more years. I envy her. By tacit agreement, neither one of us ever brings up what happened that day in the pool. When it does finally come up, we're in our late teens. I ask Hannah what happened but her memory is hazy. All she knows is that something bad happened under the water and it scared her enough to make her realize she needed to get away from him.

When I think back on that day and that man, I am both angry and grateful. I'm angry that it happened and left me silenced and ashamed for far too long, and I'm grateful that nothing worse has happened to me since. In comparison with many girls and women, we got off easy. And that's just plain sad.

WHAT I LEARNED FROM MY FATHER,

WHAT I LEARNED FROM *THE THING*

Brian Fanelli

As a boy, I didn't have much in common with my father. On Sundays, he had two rituals: make the pasta sauce with my mother and then park on the couch to watch the Green Bay Packers, volume cranked so loud that the sound of whistles and first downs echoed throughout the house. It is true that I had a short flirtation with football and rocked Dallas Cowboys gear when they had the dream team of Michael Irvin, Emmitt Smith, and Troy Aikman. It's easy to root for a team when you're young and that team is winning. However, my interest in football soon waned, and one of the only bonds I developed with my father involved horror movies. Frequently, on Friday nights, he took me to Blockbuster, where I roamed rows of horror movie VHS tapes and ran my fingers over the dark eyes of Jason's hockey mask or the knives of Freddy Kreuger's glove on movie sleeves. I still attribute my love of horror movies to my father. Looking back, I realize the movies my father praised often featured strong male leads, a staple of the horror film until the 1960s and 1970s wave that often had women one-up the villain, be it a demon or slasher. Some of my father's favorites always had a male survivor, who often saved the damsel in distress and made me think that I needed bulging muscles like sports stars or superheroes to be a man. Like my father's football-watching habit, they defined my definition of masculinity early on, until I was old enough to realize that I didn't have to be like that and such expectations were as unrealistic as the B-movie creature features we watched.

One of my father's favorite horror movies was *Night of the Living Dead*. Released in 1968 and filmed outside of Pittsburgh, the film did have its progressive moments. It featured a black male lead, for one, and its scenes of zombies gnawing human flesh were quite taboo for the time, years before *The Walking Dead* made gore and splatter a prime-time feature. *Night of the Living Dead* also had a shoe-string budget and became one of the most defining films of the horror genre. That said, for all of its liberal moments that reflected the spirit of the 1960s, it is not a progressive film in terms of gender roles or its portrayal of masculinity. Its central female character, Barbara (Judith O'Dea), spends much of the film either shrieking or mute after her relative is killed by a zombie during their trip to the cemetery in the opening sequence. She doesn't have a single moment of transformation into a bad-ass zombie killer. Until she's devoured, Barbara spends much of her on-screen time hiding out in a home with the protagonist, Ben (Duane Jones), who not only tells her to hush up, but smacks her to silence her. Watching that scene as a kid, I winced at the crack of his palm against her cheek. However, Ben was an early symbol of masculinity to me. Though he didn't have the body mass of Green Bay Packers all-stars, he was strong enough and smart enough to fend of zombies. He sniped them with ease, knocking them off one by one with a shotgun. In that way, he reminded me of a father, who was a hunter and good with a gun. Unlike Barbara, Ben didn't emote, and I wanted his survival skills. His only downfall was his skin color and the community's regressive views, which is why rednecks trying to restore law and order shoot him in the head in the last moments of the film, before burning his body. Director George A. Romero would later remedy his conservative portrayal of gender roles in *Night of the Living Dead* by writing strong female leads in *Dawn of the Dead* and *Day of the Dead*, but those weren't the films I watched with my father. I didn't see them until much later. As a boy, Ben was one of the only examples I had.

Another one of my father's favorite films was *The Thing*, 1982. This John Carpenter remake of a 1950s sci-fi classic, *The Thing from Outer Space*, tells the story of an all-male research team hauled up in artic bunkers. They contract an alien life form after discovering remains of another research team. One by one, they succumb, either through invasion of the body or distrust among each other. The film's star is R.J. MacReady, aka Mac, played by Kurt Russell. The thick-bearded Mac spends a decent amount of the film swigging whiskey and figuring out whose body is playing host to something foreign. Like Ben, Mac was another early example of masculinity to me. Once the men start dying, Mac takes charge. He tests their blood, blow torches the alien in human form, and defeats the beastie in the closing sequence by setting bombs inside the bunkers. Even during the explosions and ka-booms, he still manages to survive. Like Ben, he never cowers or backs down. He's also similar to Ben in the fact that as everything goes to hell, he keeps his cool and takes charge, falling into that stereotypical archetype of the male action hero.

While I can understand my father's like for *The Thing* and his fondness for the Kurt Russell-type action hero, I liked the film for another reason, and even today, it remains one of my favorite horror films. *The Thing* is very much a film about the body, about being alien among a group and what can happen as a result. It's no accident that Carpenter cast all men for the film. As soon as one of them starts showing signs of weakness or acts differently, they are shunned from the group, accused of being the alien, and either blow torched or locked in a shed outside of the bunkers, in negative degree temperatures, until the good guys are certain that the alien isn't inside of the bloodstream. Like all good horror movies, *The Thing* is about the other, about something outside of our social constructs that threatens the norm. In the end, Mac and another character, Childs, survive, but the rest of the men are dead, proving what happens when we start turning on each other and are quick to judge so fast.

I related to *The Thing* and still do so much because I was never a Kurt Russell-type hero. Whiskey still burns my throat and stomach. I never fired a rifle, and I certainly can't mirror any of Mac's action stunts in the closing 20 minutes. The film pushes towards something deeper. As a boy, I felt alien, trying to fit into notions of masculinity, prone to ideas of what my body should look like and how I should act.

I thought I had to be like my father, a sports fanatic who was also a star athlete in high school. I, however, flunked out of a number of sports. For a few years, I played baseball, but fed up with playing outfield and striking out, I quit. I played football at local parks with friends, but I was typically picked last because of my poor skills. I refused to even tackle anyone because I didn't like contact, and I certainly didn't want to catch the ball because I didn't want to be knocked to the ground. The one sport I excelled at, at least for a short period, was basketball, a game that isn't about the contact. You can be good at basketball, or at least some aspects of the game, by practicing. For hours and hours, I trekked to local parks to perfect foul shots, three pointers, and a quick dribble. When my father installed a b-ball hoop in my grandmother's yard, I played from after school until dusk, until my palms caked with dust and orange residue from the ball. As I sunk shot after shot, I imagined myself a type of hero, the one to sink the game-winning three to a cacophony of applause. If I couldn't be Mac or Ben, I could at least be a basketball star. They were good with a shotgun or blow torch, and I was good at sinking jumpers.

I could rebound well, too, and that skill earned me a starting center spot on a local league team. Finally, it seemed, I had won my father's approval. I scored a few points a game, blocked shots, and snagged rebounds. It helped that my growth spurt occurred early, so I had a few inches on a lot of my friends, thus making the center position my destiny. My father encouraged my love of the game by driving me two hours to see my favorite team, the Orlando Magic, face off against the Philadelphia Sixers.

However, by middle school, my dreams of being the next Penny Hardaway were dashed. I choked in tryouts, banked every free throw, and couldn't sink uncontested layups. Around the jocks, I knew that I had no long-term future in sports. Besides, I stopped growing by 8th grade, and most of the guys on the team had a few inches over me and could snatch rebounds much easier than I could by that point. Pretty soon, I stopped attending basketball games with my father and quit the sport all together.

In time, I found my voice and strength through writing, and

before my father died of cancer, he was pleased that I wrote articles for my school newspaper and was attending a good state school for comparative literature and journalism. He must have learned that I wasn't going to be the type of son he may have initially wanted, or that I initially thought I had to be. I never followed him in the woods to hunt, and I never sat in front of the tube with him on Sundays to watch the Packers. We had our horror movie nights, and for that, I'm grateful. He passed that love on to me, and the genre has certainly grown more progressive since my father's favorite flicks showed on the silver screen. Whenever I view *The Thing* now and watch Mac down his whiskey, I think of my father, rooting for the male lead to conquer the big, bad evil. I, however, still see a different point to the film, a warning about what can happen when we try to fit others into narrow definitions, including tightly defined notions of masculinity. We start turning on each other and othering each other. That's a lesson my father may not have intended, but it came through those horror movie nights with him.

CURRENCY

Marissa McNamara

I'm 16 and Alan is 18. He drives a rusted-out blue Chevelle and can barely reach the gas pedal because he is short and the car is big. We drink and smoke a lot of pot. After six months together, I lose my virginity to him. I thought he'd been waiting patiently because he loved me, but I found out later that he'd been having sex with other people the whole time. I found this out when I discovered that I had an STD, only at the time, I told myself he'd gotten it before he met me. And that could have been. But now I don't think so.

We had sex at parties. We'd disappear into random bedrooms or take a sleeping bag outside. This time we were up the street at Tommy's house. It was summer, Led Zeppelin's "Dazed and Confused" blasting on the stereo while people played pool and made out. Tommy's parents weren't home. We'd already had sex once in their bed.

There is a photo of me: my eyes half open in a haze of smoke, blond hair teased, big and sprayed into place. I'm wearing small, tight black jeans, which I starved and puked my way into. Other girls are jealous of how I look. We are in the kitchen, Tony and Tracy, and me and Alan—three or four others—with our arms around each other holding cigarettes and Budweisers and acting cool for the camera. Alan is stoned, his small, dark eyes glazed, and he wears a gray t-shirt with the sleeves cut off, worn Levi's, and scuffed brown boots, just like the other cool boys who party.

Then he took my hand, we left the party, and he led me across the front lawn. I remember the damp grass and the humid night. He took me to the car. Pressed me up against the door, and kissed me.

"I love you," he said. "Do you love me?"

"Yes, I love you, I love you, I love you," I repeated it like he always wanted.

He opened the car door, and we slid into the back seat. The world spun, and the streetlights were hazy through the windows. I loved him so much, loved how his breath smelled sweet in the morning after a night of drinking whiskey, loved how he'd pick me up after school, the car rumbling outside in the parking lot, how he'd hand me a beer, and we'd go back to his parents' empty house. He unzipped his jeans and pulled mine down to my ankles, and then he was in me, the full weight of his body pressing down on mine, my face buried in his neck, in his long hair that smelled of sweat and summer.

And then I heard it. Muffled voices. I opened my eyes to a group of boys, maybe three or four, standing at the window, staring into the steamy car, watching Alan's bare ass as he pumped me in the hazy light. One was Chip from my chemistry class. The others were boys from school.

He didn't pause. He looked up at them and kept fucking my body on the blue vinyl back seat. Something inside of me knew that the boys had been invited to watch. Something inside of me knew that Alan had known they were there. Something inside of me pushed the knowing away and let him fuck me until he came and zipped his jeans and walked me back to the party. That night became a drunk story I decided I'd imagined.

When we got back to the house, the boys gone, the show over, Tommy's father was home, but the party kept going. He walked up and handed Alan's wallet to him. He'd left it in Tommy's parents' bed. They didn't look at me. They looked at each other, a quick grin of recognition between them. My body stood there, part of the transaction, the currency exchanged when a boy becomes a man.

WATER

Megan Culhane Galbraith

It was summer, 1985. My parents had dropped me off at Camp Lohikan in the Poconos. It was a typical sleep-away summer camp. Pristine Lake Como, dotted with the colorful sails of bobbing Minifish, lay nestled between mountains of mature pines. The winding wooded hill opposite the lake was marked with brown cabins, a mess hall, tennis courts, riding stables, and the A-framed Camp Director's office, which was the only place you could make a phone call (from the rotary phone on the wall) or buy soda in a can.

I'd taken the job as a camp counselor that year after being recruited at a summer job fair at Penn State. I was a freshman trying for a summer with the Peace Corp (turns out they didn't want an orchestra nerd turned journalism major). Instead, I wound up teaching horseback riding to pre-teens.

On the verge of 19, I arrived that summer dressed in turquoise and pink Jams—the official shorts of the mid-80s—an emerald green polo shirt with the collar flipped, and mid-calf L.L. Bean duck boots.

We counselors learned about each other at orientation. We sat cross-legged in a circle on the open grass outside the mess hall and went slowly clockwise, prodded by the camp director, sharing a little bit about ourselves. There was a heavy-set black guy studying to be a mortician. A wiry, pimply kid who liked skateboarding and comic books and who took to following me around, my friend Richie who was like everyone's brother; Belinda an education major from Elmira College; Lesley, a troubled college dropout and fellow riding instructor; and Mike and Barb who would become a couple that summer. And then there was Charlie, who kept me guessing.

He was older, mid-20s perhaps. I guessed ex-Army. He was quiet, watchful. He wore cutoff jean shorts frayed just above the knee, lug sole boots, a t-shirt, and a canvas army green jacket. He carried his coffee mug everywhere. His left thumb hooked through the handle and his palm cradled the base. His hair was dark brown, shaggy and shiny. It fell over his aviator sunglasses and below his ears. He pushed it back behind his right ear before taking a swig from his mug.

We'd arrived a week before the camp kids were scheduled to be there in order to get our cabins and the barn ready. My job was to prepare the horse stalls, do general maintenance around the barn, clean tack, and break in the horses when they arrived. The heat and humidity of the Pennsylvania forest made us sweaty and sticky, but the promise of a breeze on damp skin, or the lake water at the end of the day was a simple satisfaction. Most of the time I was happily half-covered in a gritty film of musky horse dander and shavings.

I'd taken to wearing a pair of grey running shorts to do the barn work. They were lightweight with built-in panties that I soaked through daily with sweat. Over the course of the summer, they became my favorite shorts. Because of the hard work and all the riding, they'd begun to hang more loosely on my body. I'd begun to like the feel of my hipbones jutting from beneath the cool fabric and I as I walked across the field to the barn in the morning I'd taken to running my hands over my hips and ass. I was beginning to feel contours I liked.

I'd rinse the shorts out in the cabin sink every night, but not before holding them to my face, inhaling my own tangy scent.

Because of the relentless heat, I'd sometimes wear the shorts riding instead of my heavy jeans. I'd squeeze my damp thighs into borrowed suede chaps and zip them down the outside of my legs, tucking the silky ends of the shorts into the suede, which began at my upper thighs. It wasn't a foolproof strategy. In the blazing sun, at a posting trot, the shorts gathered in all my cracks and exposed my bare ass to the hot leather of the saddle. It felt ruinous and delicious all at once.

Sometimes I'd catch Charlie watching from the opposite end of the outdoor ring. He'd lean on the top rail of the fence with his arms crossed and one boot hooked over the bottom rail. On really hot days he wore a red bandana around his forehead, occasionally mopping the sweat from his mustache and beard with the back of his hand.

It was a near full moon, and six of us counselors met at the lake to go skinny-dipping. We were already a month into camp and it was our night off. Mike and Barb, and Belinda and Richie were coupled up by then, which left Charlie and me. I can't remember whose idea the skinny-dipping was, but it seemed like a challenge we were all up for; like group nakedness was some sort of necessary camp ritual. I was excited and terrified to be naked in front of other people. We stood on the beach in a silhouetted line waiting for the first person to strip and run into the water.

Richie and Belinda shed their clothes quickly, and raced ahead splashing and yelling. Richie yelled something about shrinkage. Mike and Barb stripped and followed immediately. I was left standing with Charlie on the beach, fully clothed.

"That a ring on your toe?" he said.

I looked down at my feet, "Yeah, it's been there since high school."

"Won't it come off in the water?"

"Nah."

"Kinky," he said.

I looked at him.

"You going in?" he asked.

"Planning on it."

I'd been planning how to gracefully undress with the group so as not to be studied. I both hated and wanted eyes on my body. Now, I felt exposed and singled out. I was fighting an eating disorder, which is to say fighting the myth of having the perfect body, or ever feeling comfortable in the body I had. The binge/purge cycle had intensified freshman year, but I'd begun swimming every day in the natatorium and it was meditative. Water has a way of smoothing everything out and making you feel weightless. At the time, feeling weightless in my body was a goal, but so was the urge to disappear altogether and I was well on my way. I'd lost nearly thirty pounds.

In what felt like one movement, I pulled my running shorts down, my T-shirt over my head, and unclasped my bra dropping everything in a heap. I waded into the lake up to my knees and dove in an arc, ass to the moon and the night air. The water felt like silk against my skin. It made my nipples hard. Underwater, I ran my hands over my hips, waist, and erect breasts feeling slim and powerful.

I surfaced; hair plastered to my head and turned to the beach. "You coming?" His shirt was half off and he was stepping out of his sneakers as he walked toward the water.

I began swimming to the dock in the middle of the lake, following the others. We formed a dotted line of dark wet heads bobbing in the glimmering water. I heard Charlie wade in, and then a splash. I could sense him following.

The water felt clean and cool against my skin and I kicked the breaststroke kick—balls of my feet together, knees out, my body buoyant in the lake water, naked yet hidden. Making it to the dock, I realized Charlie had closed the distance and was right behind me. When I reached up to grab the silver rails of the ladder, his hands fell into place just below mine. I leaned back into his chest and felt an electric jolt of flesh-on-flesh. His chin grazed my collarbone.

"Help you up?" he said in my ear.

I froze for a second, embarrassed to realize the full view he'd be getting from below. I curved forward and pulled myself up in one motion. I folded myself down near the ladder and stretched out flat on my back, curling my arms behind my head. My heart pounded. My ass and shoulder blades warmed against the dock, my breasts pointed hard at the night sky.

"Nice bush," Richie said.

I tried to punch him, but scraped my knuckles on the sandpapery dock.

Charlie pulled himself silently up the ladder. He walked close beside me shaking cold beads of water from his hair. He lay down behind my head where I couldn't see him. I looked up at the moon and crossed my right leg over my left at the ankles. My stomach was flat, and for a moment I admired the indent my hipbones created around the soft flesh of my belly, as if it were a pale lake between low mountains.

We talked and laughed, and gossiped about the camp director, whom we agreed probably had a coke habit, and about how sad we were for the kids whose parents dropped them there for the entire summer. Someone suggested we play the game where you lay the back of your head on another person's stomach forming a human chain link so we did that. Then someone told a ridiculous joke and our heads bumped up and down from laughter, which caused even more laughter. I don't remember Charlie participating, but I sensed him listening and watching.

In between, I silently marveled at the moon and how it made the lake water roil. I stole glimpses of the others' naked bodies, mostly triangles of dark hair and luminescent breasts, before rolling on my stomach and giving the moon the moon.

Back on shore, we toweled off, put our clothes back on and gathered in the lifeguard shed where they stored the oars, life jackets, buoys, and the thin, fiberglass hulls of sailboats. Someone had started a fire in an old coffee can with nail holes punched in the side. The shed doors were open; beer cans littered the dirt floor. The others were coupled up with their legs entwined, talking, drinking, and laughing in the flickering light.

I was sitting close to Charlie on the overturned hull of a Minifish. I was in my t-shirt and running shorts, but my bra was still out on the sand. I was shivering a bit, and my hair was wet and beginning to curl.

The other two couples fell to silent kissing. It felt awkward. Charlie leaned closer to me, "Wanna make out?"

"Mmmmm," I said.

I leaned my left shoulder under his right arm, but he maneuvered me to lie down on his lap facing him. The lower half of my body was still on the boat hull and my knees were bent. I didn't know what to do with my right arm, so I encircled his waist, sliding my palm up his back under his shirt. "Sorry about my cold hand," I said tracing the jut of each backbone with my fingers and shivering.

Cradling the back of my neck in the crook of his left arm, he pulled me up to meet his mouth. I paused and breathed him in. He kissed me slowly and gently; I tasted the faint trace of a cigarette smoked possibly hours ago. My tongue tracked his mustache where it met his top lip. Our teeth clicked together and I laughed pulling back. "Sorry," I said. He parted me with his tongue. I moved deeper into him and his right hand slipped under my shirt and up my ribcage, his thumb tracing the underside of my left breast before he fanned his fingers out, cupping it from the side and swirling his forefinger around my pointed nipple.

"You're a handful," he said.

I kissed him deeper and squirmed. Planting my right hand on the sailboat hull for balance, I took my mouth off his and brought my left hand up to his cheek. His still-damp hair was soft and I lifted my body up to kiss his forehead, working my way slowly down to his eyelids, cheekbones, and chin before burying my face at the indentation at the base of his neck inhaling him. I licked beads of lake water from his hair before searching again for his mouth. His palm was at the small of my back now, pressing me into him. We curled around each other. I'd have kept kissing him like that forever. I felt desirable, lit, devoured.

The shed felt like it was swimming around me. I could hear the whimper and crackle of the tiny can fire, and the others whispering to each other and laughing softly. Here I am, I thought, I'm *in* my body. I *like* my body. I like what's being done to my body, and what I'm doing to someone else's body.

Charlie's right hand was now on the soft round of my belly. He moved it slowly down and around toward my ass and down my thigh. He worked his fingers up under my shorts tracing the outline of my hip, mirroring the curve of the panties with his thumb on my goose bumped skin. I couldn't control my wetness. I shuddered and smelled my own embarrassed heat. I let out a nearly inaudible noise, from deep in the back of my throat; the same sound I make now when I hear a delicious poem I want to fuck. He pulled me tighter.

"Let's get outta here," he said.

He stood and extended his hand to help me up. Barefoot and flushed, I tugged my T-shirt down, straightened my shorts, and felt his stare. We went outside to his brown Ford Pinto. I chattered nervously about spending summers tooling around with my friend in her brother's Pinto, and "Aren't these the cars with the gas tank that catches fire?" and "Do you have any good cassettes? What kind of music do you like to listen to?"

When I was settled in the front seat, he put the car into gear.

"Where do you want to go," he asked.

"I don't care," I said. "What do you mean?"

"Well, we can't go back to the cabins," he said.

I shrugged.

He looked at me and cocked his head. "Have you ever had sex?"

I looked down into my own wet lap.

"God damn, girl" he said. "I'm not going to be your first, but what are you doing kissing someone like that if you had no intentions of following through?"

I looked at his crotch, tented in his jean shorts.

Oh, but I'd *had* intentions.

Up until then I'd never even had a boyfriend. I'd spent my high school years focused on the negatives about my body—hips and thighs that didn't fit traditional Levi's; not having a 24-inch waist like many of my friends; a robust derriere that came between me and wearing Calvin Klein jeans—that I'd never considered I was capable of turning someone on. I hadn't realized my body's power back then; or how to use it to give myself pleasure; or that I deserved pleasure; or that deep kissing and heavy petting wasn't an end in itself, but a gateway drug to desire. I was too busy punishing myself for existing; too busy putting food in my mouth out of self-loathing instead of nourishment, and then throwing it up in shame. I'd wasted so many years on the nostalgic regret that is negative self-talk; on trying to fix my outer self instead of just *being* myself. In all of this remembering, I most wanted

117

to go back to my freckled, teenaged self and give her a goddamned do-over.

Had I known then what I know now, I would have suggested to Charlie that we meet back at the shed after everyone had left. I'd have pushed him down onto the overturned Minifish, straddled his hips and leaned his back against the rib of the shed wall. I'd have held his gaze with mine, pulled my T-shirt slowly over my head, leaned back and offered myself up to his hot mouth. He'd hold me behind the shoulder blades and begin just below my ribs, moving slowly upward. I'd arch my back, put my hands on his knees and let him devour me until we were feverish and breathing hard.

I'd grab a handful of his hair and pull him close. I'd bend forward to meet his mouth, kiss him as if I were surfacing to breathe in the lake, and gently bite his lower lip. I'd curl my fingers into his and place his hands on my body exactly where it felt good. I'd tug his shorts open.

"Please," I'd say, grazing his ear with my lips. "Oh, please."

With my thumb, I'd move aside the panties in my running shorts and slip him inside me, silky and wet. We'd swirl around each other, listening to the lake lap the shore outside. His hands guiding my hips; the water outside reminding us that it always finds its own level.

THE WOUND
Vicki Addesso

When I saw them—the first few hairs, dark, the longest a half inch—I was confused, then scared. This was down where I peed. I wondered if more would grow, when they would stop. I checked each morning. When I saw that one seemed to be coming from inside, I decided to put an end to it.

I waited until night. I locked the bathroom door. My mother's tweezers were in the medicine cabinet. I had often watched as she plucked her eyebrows, standing in front of the mirror wincing. I took off my pajama bottoms, sat on the floor, legs spread on the cold tiles. I hunched over as far as I could. I took one of the hairs between the tweezers' points and pulled. The skin rose with the hair. It hurt. I kept pulling and then, squeezing the tweezers as tight as I could, tore it away. A small dot of blood appeared; I blew the ugly hair into the toilet. The pain had been terrible, but that was okay, for there was the after-pain, the ache that soothed with the assurance that the worst was over.

I found my mother's hand-mirror in a drawer below the sink and positioned it between my thighs, working quickly. I grabbed the hair that was growing from inside of me. I looked closely in the mirror. I hesitated. I let go of the tweezers, stood, and holding the mirror with one hand I opened my flesh wider with the other.

Pieces of skin—shiny, purple, ragged, sloppy—hung limp from inside their hiding place. Layers inside layers. It had to be a mistake, a deformity. This was a wound.

I let go of myself, put the mirror and tweezers away, and washed my hands. Lying in bed, I cupped the injured area with my left hand, over my pajamas, and pressed gently, hoping I had not made it worse.

I let the hair grow. It grew thick, but not longer, hiding the wound well. After my shower it curled into springy ringlets. Later, it would lie matted and flat, pressed by tight jeans.

Soon, I began to scratch myself. At night, in bed, in the dark. In spots that no one could see. My thighs, my stomach. I scratched a small spot until the blood would rise to just below the surface in lacy designs, the skin marbled, enough of it scraped away that I could feel the moistness of a newly exposed layer. It was the warm after-pain I was waiting for. The ache of it being over.

When I started punching myself, I realized something must be wrong with me. Still, in my bed, lights out, the house quiet, I'd do it. I would make a fist, I would let the knuckle of my middle finger jut out, and I'd hit my cheekbone, over and over again. At the point when I thought I couldn't stand it, when it hurt so much I wanted to stop, I kept going. I would check, run my fingertips over the spot, feel the puffiness, the swelling, feel the tiny pillow I had made over my bone. Sometimes I would wake up to see that there was no evidence of my self-inflicted pain; I would feel disappointed for stopping too soon. But if I'd done it right, the spot would be swollen and bruised. I did not hide the damage. When anyone asked, I'd say I bumped into a door, or a book fell off the shelf. My father didn't notice, as he had stopped looking at me months ago. Friends called me clumsy. But my mother—why didn't she question me further?

For my twelfth birthday, in March, my mother gave me a training bra. As my friends got their periods and bragged about it, I waited for mine. One morning in July I woke with an ache in my abdomen. Walking to the bathroom I saw that my underpants were stained red. I called for my mother. She had tears in her eyes as she showed me how to put on the elastic belt and attach a sanitary napkin. She seemed nervous, but happy. I worried that she would be shocked by the hair that had grown down there, but she didn't mention it.

Later that summer, I was at a friend's house.

"Let's listen to music. We can borrow some of my brother's albums."

I followed her downstairs, to her older brother's basement room.

The blue walls were covered with posters, taped crookedly, of rock bands and girls in bikinis. The bed was unmade; clothes were thrown all over the floor. She told me he was at work, and she opened the closet door, reaching in to pull out the old milk crates filled with record albums. A picture hung inside the door.

In the picture a young woman is smiling, lying on a bed, propped up on satin pillows, naked. Her legs are spread open, her right hand reaches down, her fingers pull open the lips between her legs. I see it. Shiny, wet, and the skin inside folds and twirls around itself.

That night I locked the bathroom door. I found my mother's mirror. I sat on the floor, I spread my legs, I opened myself up again. I hadn't looked since that first time. I saw that I was the same. The same as the girl in the picture. We all must have it, I thought. The same wound.

I scratched and hit myself less often. Eventually I stopped. I was growing up. I was learning new ways to hurt myself.

SCARS

Beverly Donofrio

When I was 17, a thyroidectomy left an angry ¼-inch-wide scar that traversed the front half of my neck, a slash, with little dots above and below from the clamps the surgeon used. Home from the hospital, I sobbed in the mirror for days that turned into weeks, because I thought I looked like Frankenstein, was now a freak, would never be a model or a movie star, and my life was totally ruined.

It didn't take long for the dots to fade, but for years people stared at my neck as we spoke, their eyes flitting between my eyes and the scar. To the few who asked how I got the scar, I explained that a surgeon had cut out most of my enlarged thyroid gland.

But a decade down the road, I preferred to say, "I slit my throat with a broken Coke bottle," which didn't feel like a lie to me but just another way of saying—metaphorically speaking—what had really happened: I got pregnant in the 12th grade by a high school drop-out, who I decided I loved after he wept one night on my shoulder, saying, "I'm no good. You shouldn't love me." I had the thyroid operation because I was soon pregnant by the aforementioned, self-proclaimed no-gooder, and the radioactive iodine used those days to treat overactive thyroids would have harmed the baby. Fact is, my unwanted motherhood—not the glaring Scarlet Letter of a scar—was the honest-to-goodness reason I believed my life was ruined.

In the Hindu tradition, the throat is the fifth chakra, the seat of communication. Before I got pregnant, I had no problem speaking my mind. In junior high—or what's now called middle school—and again in high school, I was most teachers' worst nightmare, what my Father-the-Cop liked to call a Smart Mouth. But I like to think my mother, whom I called my father's slave, silently admired my courage.

At my mother's wake, my sisters and I had the opportunity to ask our seventh-grade English teacher how he remembered us. He nodded at the youngest, "Janet, you were a free spirit." To the middle sister, "Pat, you were a good student, hardworking, studious." And to me, "I was afraid of you." And he had reason to be. I said what I thought. I did not hold back. I asked tough questions, and I would defend my convictions against anything or anyone. I knew no one else who had an innate drive like mine—the need to give voice to what other people might be thinking but were too polite or frightened to say out loud.

But that was before I became a teen mother. While I was pregnant, I developed the overactive thyroid, also known as a goiter, which presented as a lump on my throat. At seventeen and raised Catholic, I believed my pregnancy a punishment for my societally-unsanctioned behavior: sex too young and out-of-wedlock. And I think the goiter was a physical manifestation of how ashamed and guilty I felt: censored and wrong, wrong thinking and wrong speaking. A lump in my belly and another in my throat. The thyroid is a butterfly-shaped gland that is situated just behind the voice box. A goiter can interfere with speech. I believe I was so humiliated; I gave myself a goiter to choke off and silence my despair. I wonder: was I so shamed that I believed I no longer had the right to speak?

Over the years, the scar on my neck has faded and no one notices it anymore. But decades before it faded, back in my late-thirties, I stopped seeing it when I looked in a mirror. It became as much a part of me as the nose on my face. The Scarlet Punctuation Mark was no longer important; it did not define me. By then, I'd had years of therapy and had been given the great gift of a contract to write my first book, in which I gave myself permission, and indeed was paid money, to be as truthful as I could be and to say exactly what I thought. In *Riding in Cars with Boys* I railed against sexism; the Catholic Church, the times and the society I grew up in—the unrepentantly repressive 1950s—for attempting to condition me to be obedient and compliant, a good, nice, respectful girl, who keeps her big mouth shut. Finishing that book, speaking my truth, I felt exonerated.

Sometimes I imagine going through the tunnel people who have had near-death experiences describe, heading toward the light, looking back at my life, and suddenly everything is connected to everything else—a big dot-to-dot picture, an image, maybe like a beautiful mandala, that will make sense out of my entire life. That scar that made me look like someone had chopped off my head and sewn it back on will be connected to the stretch marks on my hips from gaining 70 pounds while I was pregnant, and those stretch marks will be connected to the dark patch on my shoulder where it slid along the concrete sidewalk last summer when I tripped in Brooklyn, excited and in a rush to see my grandkids.

In that bright light, I'll understand how the burn and cut scars on my hands are connected to the burn and cut scars on my mother's hands, which I'd stared at in disgust when she was in her fifties and I in my still-vain thirties. I'll see her at the kitchen table, as she once sat, drinking her first pot of coffee of the morning, complaining about her sinuses, her allergies, her swollen ankles, aching back, her mother-in-law, the weather, and I across the table, fixated on her newest scar, which blisters on the rim of her palm after bumping against the hot oven while pulling out a lemon meringue pie. I believe my mother's scars were an emblem of the way she lived her life: burnt and in pain. The spiritual teacher Adyashanti says, "It's an alchemical miracle that our bodies can be duplicators of our thoughts." Perhaps scars are the body's voice.

Even before the enlightenment that I envision flowing as I fly through that tunnel, here and now, at sixty-six, I know that having my son was one of the greatest blessings in my life and that all the scars my body has made, and will make in the future, are the surest proof of, not past mistakes and wounds, but of healing. I feel very lucky to have lived long enough to observe that some scars actually disappear.

It helps to rub them with Vitamin E oil, which at this moment I am doing as I plan my response to the next person who, taken aback by something I've said, responds sarcastically—like so many have done before: "Why don't you tell us what you *really* think, Bev." To which I will say, "Why the hell would I do anything else?"

Except, perhaps, if I shut my mouth out of kindness, an attribute I would do well to develop—but I'm thinking I may wait till I'm 70.

THE UBIQUITOUS BODY
Renée Ashley

Just hours after I received the invitation to write about body image, I came across "The Grammar Is on You," a poem by Nate Pritts, in *The Literary Review*. The opening's head-smacking insight took me by surprise; I've never been able to state it so concisely, so perfectly, myself. He says:

> The fact of my body separate from other bodies
> Separate but in sight of in context with.

My body in the context of other bodies: the fat girl's dilemma. So foundational, so inescapable. I had stopped thinking about it. The fish-in-water parable, unambiguous and spot-on. I have no idea where that parable began, but David Foster Wallace's version goes like this: "There are these two young fish swimming along, and they happen to meet an older fish swimming the other way, who nods at them and says, 'Morning, boys, how's the water?' And the two young fish swim on for a bit, and then eventually one of them looks over at the other and goes, 'What the hell is water?'"

That's exactly how conditioned by and how distanced from I'd become by what was going on around me——the steady bombardment of demands to squeeze my own body into the context of the mannequin bodies paraded and promoted before me by a constant media and social barrage that insists on comparison. That's the water I'm swimming in, and it's fitted out to make me feel bad about my body.

Within a day or so of reading the Pritts poem, I found an interview with Max Ritvo in my in-box. Ritvo was twenty-five, and

126

dying of cancer. "My body seems, on the face of it," he said, "to be the main thing for me! But somewhere along the line I've learnt my body is basically a giant nutrient and blood supply."

My body seems ...to be the main thing for me. It seemed that Pritts and Ritvo—whose pieces were working in concert in my head now—had led me to tap into my sublimated body issues: that not only do I see my body as inferior, but I think about it constantly in the context of other bodies. At its least, my body has become the basket I carry myself in. At its worst, the bag they'll tie me up in when I'm done.

I'd thought—I really had—that, long ago, I'd at least come to terms with my body. I've never loved it. And, if I ever hated it, somewhere along the line, I'd managed to let that go. It was just *my body*—the way, when you're very young, your mom is *just* your mom. Though my body was, and at times still is, a frustration, a too-bright spotlight on my failure to meet the norms of beauty that compounds my other feelings of social inadequacy, I had become habituated.

But fifty years ago, late in high school, I wasn't so numb to it. I starved myself to lose weight for an upcoming, entire-weekend date with a gorgeous man twice my age. I had eaten almost nothing for a week. He picked me up and off we went to his rustic home in the foothills. He made scallop stew, a cream-based dish, rich with butter and wine, and while he stirred, and moved about his kitchen in a practiced, sexy way, we talked and laughed while we picked at cheeses and grapes, and drank yet another glass of white wine. When we sat down to eat—at the intimate, elegant table he'd laid—I dipped the silver spoon into the fabulous stew, raised it to my mouth, and abruptly vomited both into my bowl and across the tiny table where my stream of spew was split by the single long-stemmed rose in the silver vase. When I could raise my eyes, my unsmiling date was still wiping at his hands and shirt cuffs with his water-dipped, linen napkin. I was bundled up like a sack of dirty laundry—which I definitely was—and delivered back to my mother's house before the clock had struck eight p.m.

I never dieted-to-the-extreme again. Dieted, yes, and miserably, no doubt—but never again like that. Whether that was because I had learned my lesson or, simply, because it never again seemed important enough to me, isn't clear. But when I happen on photos from that time, I think, *What on earth was my problem?*

I was clearly at odds with my body, but not so much at odds that I ever again knocked myself out trying to change it. The compulsion never took hold of me as it did some of my svelter friends, one of whom kept repeating, "That growling in your stomach is your body eating away at your fat" until I wanted to kill her. If the body's a temple, as some believe, it was pretty clear I'd dedicated mine to a dissolute god, otiose and unmindful.

Now, my body is my mother's body: same blue eyes, same sun-starved skin, same big, open pores on my nose, same breasts, same vertical ridges in my thumbnails and the nails of my ring fingers, same lack of waistline, same thick, yellow calluses that build up quickly on the outside edges of my big toes. Even the same late-in-life gallbladder surgery and the same turkey wattle beneath my chin.

During most of my life, my mother and I were at odds, and now I've become my adversary's doppelganger—and I think I am at odds with the her in me, as well. Yet, my body has always been a hospitable one. It's a big body, I'll give it that, but it's neither broken nor prone to illness. Granted, I've fractured my nose a handful of times, so that, now, it meanders a bit on my face; and follow-up plastic surgery from a small skin cancer left a baker's-twine-thick, doubly-loopy scar along my nasal ridge; and my gallbladder's been removed, leaving five small scars on my belly. Each even the tiniest bit disfiguring, yes, but nothing approaching monstrous. In the last few decades, I've managed my body as a necessary condition of life—as Max Ritvo'd pointed out: "a giant nutrient and blood supply." Unconsciously, I think, I began to consider it, at best, a vehicle. Clean and presentable and mobile would do fine. It didn't have to be fancy; fancy takes too much upkeep and I'm an impatient woman. It simply had to get me where I was going and not shame me in any immediate functional or fluid way.

So, I was astonished, in a review of my most recent book, *The View from the Body*, to see so many quotes pulled *about* the body; after all, the view *from* a body does not, under normal circumstances, include the

128

body doing the viewing. But there was, it was pointed out to me, a deluge of *body*s in the work: "The body: deluded, distressed, its incontestable world / loose in the other world," a "body named/bone, named brain," "[b]ag of flesh, suck of roiling guts-- / is that you?" and the tell-all high notes: "She is trying to get out of her body" and the epigraph, "Body, maybe, is the only word the body knows." Son of a gun. *So much for having come to terms with my body.*

I admit, I still catch myself, every once in a while, surveying a room to determine whether I'm the fattest person in it. Sometimes I'm not, and, as awful as it sounds, I'm somewhat relieved; most often, though, I am, and that's also become a bit of a stress-reducer because then it's settled. I've been there before and nothing horrible happened. Evidently there are days I just need to place myself in relation to others—am I just punishing myself?—so that then I can stop assessing that water I'm in, just about put it out of my mind, and get on with business. But the evidence clearly shows I haven't been putting it as far "out of my mind" as I thought.

Since shame, for a lot of reasons, was a family staple as I grew up, it's no real surprise I inherited that along with the blue eyes and nose pores. But strong women are changing the waters of my parallel parable. Women have become more self-assured. There are plus-size models now; young women feel freer to dress as they like; and Jennifer Weiner, the novelist, recently wrote, in the *New York Times* about putting on her size sixteen bathing suit, having her husband take photos, and posting them on her Facebook page. Weiner made a point of her self-consciousness, the point being, evidently, *Get over it.* And then, made a point as well, of celebrating the liberation her act had occasioned for others. Self-possession is a wonderful thing—a joy, really—to witness. Even more young women will inherit this in the future. I applaud and I aspire to it.

My imperfect body image is always operating somewhere in me, it's clear, even if it's just running, like an app, in the background. It's a constant, like the ongoing and steady microwave signal coming from all directions left over from the big bang. Which, now that I think of it, is like the waves of the media and social barrage I began this essay with, the difference being the self-image barrage continues to be an attack on us by us; the bad-body app running the background, is a by-product of that. The big bang radiation? Well, it's not likely that anybody, large or small, can do anything to remedy that. And that gives me some perspective.

The point is that there are women willing to bet on self-acceptance and I see them more and more often. And there are others—like me, older and a bit hidebound—watching them do it and win. We're progressing—the proof is out there, swimming in the parabolic waters. Some of us will break through faster than others. None of us are perfect. But we're getting stronger. And, even better, we're everywhere.

IRONMAN

Karol Nielsen

I was a naturally athletic child. I used to round up the neighborhood to play baseball, football, tether ball, hide and seek, and kick the can. I skate boarded, roller skated, ice skated, skied, and biked. I took ballet, gymnastics, horseback riding, tennis, swimming, and diving lessons. I was co-captain of my high school swim team and competed in the Connecticut state diving championships. I ran track, too.

After college, I moved to New York City and did marathons and triathlons. I swam 2.4 miles, biked 112 miles, and ran 26.2 miles—a full marathon—to become an Ironman. I did the race twice—first in flat Panama City, Florida, then in hilly Lake Placid, New York. It was fall when I did my last long ride before the first one. It was drizzling and my lips turned blue from the chill. After the ride, I popped my bike into my beat-up minivan and stopped at a deli on the way to my parents' house in Connecticut. You need lots of tender loving care when you train for an Ironman. My parents pampered me and cheered at both races.

When I got out of the minivan, two good-looking guys turned away from slim blondes and stared at me in a lustful way. I had to smile. My long, dark hair had been washed by rainwater and sweat. I didn't have makeup on and my lips were a little blue. I was in a jersey, leggings, and flip-flops. I was fit but I wasn't bone skinny. I was about the same weight I was in high school, when my diving coach said I could model if I lost 15 pounds. I didn't want to model. I wanted to use my mind for a living. I studied hard and went to a good university and became a journalist and writer and poet.

I wasn't training for the Ironman to look good. I was doing it because I wanted to know if I had what it took to finish. And I probably stepped out of the minivan with the quiet bravado of someone about to do an Ironman. It might sound cocky, but the thing about sports is that you're always getting knocked down, the way I was at the end of the race. I'd battled ocean waves on the swim, swelled from salt pills on the bike, and began the run thoroughly bloated. My thighs were shot and so was my back. I limped along like Quasimodo in *The Hunchback of Notre-Dame*. My mother spotted me at the halfway mark and called out, "Pick it up, pick it up!" I smiled at her as if drugged. I wanted to go faster but could only manage a slow hobble that I now call the Ironman shuffle. A pretty triathlete had told me at an Ironman training camp, "It's the most humiliating thing you'll ever do."

I ran with an engineer during the final miles of the marathon. He calculated exactly how fast we had to go in order to make the midnight cutoff. We made it with 15 minutes to spare. It didn't matter how long it took to finish that 140.6-mile race. When I was done, I carried the confidence of someone whose body, and ego, could endure a serious beating. It's the biggest beauty secret I know.

I didn't always know this. One of my best friends from college figured it out first. Erin was captain of the women's crew team at the University of Pennsylvania. I rowed for a while, too, but couldn't stand the pre-dawn workouts. Erin is a morning person so it worked out for her. One day, after practice, she said she noticed a strange thing. She was sweaty and her hair was a mess, but every guy along the Skukyl River stared her down like a Vegas showgirl. Erin was Amazon tall with chestnut hair down to her waist, but she didn't always get stared down like that. It was her confidence that came from rowing that made her magnetic.

When I started doing triathlons, I met an East German at a dance club. He told me he was a law student. I told him I was a writer. He said he loved American soap operas and showed me his license, a hint of eyeliner like a punk. He wanted me to know he wasn't boring. "There's something about you," he fished. "You seem strong."

I laughed. "I am strong. I'm a triathlete."

"Yes, yes, that's it," he said. "My ex-girlfriend was an Ironman."

Not long after doing the Ironman, I went for a six-mile run in Central Park, then showered and went out without makeup, wearing jeans and a t-shirt and flip flops. Men smiled and stared at me all along the sidewalk. One followed close behind. I looked back and he was sizing me up and down. He was frat-boy handsome, like the clean-cut, all-American men in my neighborhood on the east side of Central Park. Some even vote Democratic.

A little boy ran beside me during my first race. "Lady, why are you doing this?" he asked. I joked that it was for the t-shirt. And after I was done I got my medal, t-shirts, a baseball cap, a fleece vest, a water bottle, and a coffee cup with the Ironman logo. My credit card company even offered me an Ironman card. Clerks at the checkout counter sometimes thought it meant the movie franchise. I didn't always correct them, and when I did sometimes they'd go blank. Who would swim, bike, and run that far all in one day? Sometimes people stare with starry admiration when I wear my Ironman hat and shirt and fleece or say I've done the race. Sometimes they glare as if they think I wasn't fast enough or look too human to have done the race. And sometimes they correct me. "Ironwoman," they say, as if it's not ladylike to say you're an Ironman. I feel diminished by these responses, but like that long and limit-testing race, they only make me stronger.

NEW VIBE: ON PRACTICING

MYSORE ASHTANGA YOGA FOR 30 DAYS

Lucas Hunt

9/1

I forget what poses to do in what order. I know how to do them, but there is a sequence. Sweat pours from my pores. I'm counting breaths, then it starts to flow. First I feel things, then I do them. Everyone around me does the same thing, but we all do it differently. The instructor adjusts me, and it feels good. He helps me do what I can already do. I relax deep into a posture. I rinse off in the shower after practice.

9/5

Today was tough, my knees and hamstrings hurt. I'm not sure if I'm doing it right, but tried to adjust to take pressure off of the backs of my knees, especially during seated-forward bends. I struggle with the transition between seated poses, where you cross your legs, plant your hands on either side of your hips, lift your body off the ground, swing your legs back through your arms, and extend them so your body is in a push up position. Practice.

9/6

Something happened today. I was very sore, and considered taking the day off. However, I decided to go easy, and play around with things. The starting sequences felt good. I really concentrated on inhaling and exhaling, while engaging my pelvic floor and abdomen during each breath. The effects were immediate. I felt little to no stress on my knees and hamstrings. Bent over and seated postures became more about my hips, waist, and torso; the mental focus on my practice. My legs were merely the trunks of my breath. My practice became effortless. There were times my body wanted to crumble. Yet my physical exertions were nothing beside the focus on breath. My body felt good.

9/9

The studio was pretty full, and people were practicing at all different levels, many more advanced than myself. There was an attractive woman doing things behind me that I cannot do, and I got distracted. The poses felt good, and I remembered them all. I did what I could, and concentrated on *prana* (energetic breath), *drishti* (direction of the gaze) and *bhandas* (energy locks in the pelvic floor, abdomen, and throat). I wanted to practice again yesterday afternoon. I felt happy after.

9/15

The hardest day. I barely make it through practice, as my left hip flexor hurts. I try not to think the word *injury*. I breathe deeply, down my back and into the cavity of my torso, and pelvis. There is an elongation of breath and spinal fluidity during the seated postures, but transitions are tough. I have to pause and take breaths out of sequence, to focus my mind on moving forward. I wonder whether I should stop but keep going, and limp out of class. It would be fine to stop, but I want to get through the pain, to move forward with life.

9/16

A piece of skin comes off my right big toe while doing the opening sequence. It is hard to physically do the postures. I focus on breath, feel it go deeper into my body than ever before. As my physical practice evolves, it goes beyond what my mind thinks it can do. I recognize that pain and distraction pass. I speak with the instructor after class, and he says injury is the best instructor. To just wait for the pain to pass, and experience what it is like to have breath enter and exit your body.

9/25

I focus on strength, clarity, contentment and joy, and feel love in myself. Prayer, meditation, not eating at least two hours before sleep, being honest about my feelings; yoga expands into other areas of life. I took a long nap yesterday, and it was the right thing to do. I ate a big West Indian feast for lunch, with a couple of Red Stripes and cake. I take time to check in with myself, and feel good.

9/26

It may be a mistake to examine each day's practice, as if they are separate from others. There is continuity from day to day, and carry over to other things in life. What happens in between yoga is important. Yoga is a way to settle down from, and prepare for life. I notice this in my romantic world; the tendency to overthink distances me from the reality. I let thoughts settle, and feel what happens. It can be truly expressed when it comes from the heart.

9/29

Last night I did not sleep much, but woke up ready for practice. Sweat poured out, maybe from beer. I accidentally stomp on my thumb with my heel, which bruises right away. The instructor helps me into new, more advanced, seated poses. They are physically bizarre. I do not know what my body is doing, but it feels luminous. The more I breathe, the more I slip into a moving meditation.

9/30

I am sluggish because of a Trinidadian feast that I ate last night. There are things I thought that I would never be able to do, which I can now do, or am close to doing. My body is strong, supple and lithe. My heart speaks in a new way. Listening to what's going on inside, I can address what's happening outside. This is who I am.

WATER POLO
Jared Povanda

"Jared, get the ball!"

I hear the words in snippets—cut up like ribbons—as the water rushes over me. Into me. The froth batters against my lips. There's the press of many bodies, most muscular, all slick. I am sixteen and stick-thin.

They circle around me, sharks in this too-blue water, and I am spun against them, a leaf caught in decay. Chlorine bites my nose.

I hear Mrs. Russo yelling the same four words again and again, screaming at me to get the ball.

I cough, shaking as I feel my lungs heave, as my thoughts fold up in my head, over and over like a blue cloth napkin. The water burrows in my ears and I can't help but be reminded of moles and earth and earthworms.

I see the gym with bloodshot eyes: the ceiling is as gray as the sky outside the windows, and the white cement blocks of the walls stand as stoic as soldiers. As the boys we are all supposed to be. As the boy I am not. You would be able to climb the bones of my back like a ladder if you weren't afraid of touching someone whose heartbeat is visible through the skin of his chest.

Someone else has the ball now. A tall someone, an athletic someone. His movements are lupine and disciplined, as powerful as a storm.

I shouldn't be here.

The fatiguing ache doesn't move up my calves in incremental ways—it is not a dimmer switch—but all at once, a magic trick where the coin is there and then gone and then…

Hands push me deep. Too many hands. Grabbing. Pulling. Reaching. My skin is cool and hot, a playground for ghosts. Their fingertips.

I open my eyes. I drift to the surface. The sounds of the yelling boys and the yelling gym teacher are muffled, far away. Their shadows dance before me, behind me, and all around, pulling at the light. Snagging its corners and shifting it across the expanse of the water.

This is not water polo.

This is just what I would like it to be.

A game not of aggression and power, but of embrace. A game where the water drapes over limbs. Where its players float and stare and dream. No more sharks or wolf-like boys, only people swimming in a pool. The thought is sweet enough to make my teeth ache.

Mrs. Russo's words echo in my head sometimes, and I wonder if I should have just sucked it up and tried for the ball. It would have been the manly thing to do. Maybe I would have been inducted into their club of testosterone and chest hair and playful slaps on the ass.

Knowing my luck, though, I would have made a fool of myself.

I can still see that teenage me reflected in the surface of the pool. I can see the brown hair plastered in fraying clumps to my forehead. I can see my ribs, and I can feel the desire they carried to push through and out of me like wings. To take me away.

I wonder if I will ever be able to get these memories, these insecurities about my body, to drown. Maybe they'll always float to the surface of the pool belly-up. Swollen. Glassy-eyed.

Never good enough to hack it with the sharks in the deep end.

THE MAGIC OF LISTENING TO YOUR BODY
Hélène Cardona

I used to exhaust my body through sports to find peace. My mother enrolled me in ballet classes very early on to correct the way I walked because I started walking too young. This was the beginning of a love for discipline, effort, and music. In the poem "Life in Suspension" I write: "I'm six years old in ballet class in Geneva, breaking my point shoes. / The Russian master ingrains in me the correlation / between pleasure and pain. / I now know the two centers sit next to each other in the brain." I grew up dancing, skiing, swimming, running, and riding horses. As a teenager I took up Judo, and later on Tai Chi. I always felt very connected to my body. A healthy mind in a healthy body.

The body is the best barometer. The second year in medical school was the most brutal. I put that time behind me and didn't look back. I erased a couple of years from my life as if they never happened. I was mentally, emotionally, physically and spiritually drained. I remember thinking, *this is not what I'm meant to do.* I couldn't communicate, couldn't throw away a promising career, couldn't disappoint. I didn't exist. One day I simply collapsed. It was like giving up my soul. I went through a deep depression and nearly died. Which is what saved me. It was a deeply transforming spiritual experience that put me on my path. That's when I knew that who I really am never dies and is connected to something bigger and stronger than I ever knew, unconditional love, the Mystery.

The body tells me right away what's wrong. After receiving my Master's in English and American literature from the Sorbonne, I suffered from severe anemia because of overdrive. I was working as a translator/interpreter for the Canadian Embassy in Paris, studying

German, and pursuing theater at the same time. Again, something had to give.

Even though these experiences were traumatic, I consider them a gift, for they forced me to reevaluate what I was doing. They were catalysts that changed the course of my life. That's when I decided to start over, apply to the American Academy of Dramatic Arts and move to New York to pursue acting.

The search for fulfillment is a recurrent theme in my life. It's the title of the thesis I wrote about Henry James. Jean-Claude Renard writes that "I" by essence becomes "Other," that is to say "someone who not only holds the power to fulfill his or her intimate self more and more intensely, but also at the same time, can turn a *singular* into a *plural* by creating a work that causes, in its strictest individuality, a charge emotionally alive and glowing with intensity." In that sense the works' artistry affects others and helps their own transformation. It's about transcending darkness, which exists in the mind and in the world.

For me everything is experiential. It's beyond faith. The one faith I would have is faith in myself. The mysticism arose from overcoming deeply personal and traumatic experiences, tragedies, leading to a new awareness of existence. A source of life can be found within this darkness, and a presence founded on this absence. What defines my writing is the sacred dimension of the poetic experience. And it is founded in very concrete reality, a reconciliation of the spiritual and the carnal. It speaks of transformation and seeks the unison of all that lives.

Poetry is language for the ineffable, what is impossible to write, the mystery. I seek the light within that mystery. To quote Paracelsus: "There is nothing in heaven and earth which is not also in man." And the new life subsumes both death and life. We are stretched to the frontiers of what we know, exploring language and the psyche. The poem is a gesture, a movement, an opening towards a greater truth or understanding. Art brings us to the edge of the incomprehensible. Poetry and life are prayer, enchantment, transmutation of the being leading to fulfillment. The poems, in their alchemy and geology, are fragments of dreams, enigmas, shafts of light, part myth, part fable. Mysticism constitutes the experience of what transcends us while inhabiting us. Poetry, as creation, borders on it. It is metaphysical. It offers a new vision of the universe, reveals the soul's secrets and mysteries, the "other side" of what exists, to quote H.D.

I have trained with different shamans. Just like in many shamanic traditions, it is after traversing the dark night of the soul that the mystic gains spiritual vision. The past life regression therapy training I did with Tineke Noordegraaf (using the holographic model of reincarnation therapy) is a reminder of the mysteries of life and birth and rebirth. There is no duality between body and soul.

There is a certain magic that happens when I listen to my body. Now I'm more gentle with myself and do mostly yoga. When my body feels most alive, so does my mind and my whole being. I can more easily tap into other worlds, my creativity, my intuition.

BARING IT ALL
Lily Caraballo

When I called the art department at the University of Southern California, it was done more out of morbid curiosity than out of a need to make money. I felt pretty certain that I wasn't going to get the job for two reasons: I was not a professional model and I was not in the best of shape. I was surprised to find out that none of them were required when you're booked as a nude model. I was even more surprised that I had made the call in the first place.

Really, it was my friend Erick who plucked up my courage to make the call; I told him of my interest in nude modeling one time five years earlier (and seventy pounds lighter). It was listed in an article about jobs where you could make quick cash with little experience. Who doesn't want to get paid for doing nothing, especially when all you're required to do is stand still for twenty minutes? Even though I wouldn't call it a dream job of mine, it was always something that I wanted to try out.

"What's stopping you from doing it now?" he asked when I finished. I honestly had no clue. I've always been the most comfortable in my birthday suit (a fact that my mother finds very unsettling), and I already had my hands full with freelance work and school. But I hadn't found any clients in months, and I was strapped for cash. So maybe the call did reek of desperation for financial relief.

The call was short—incredibly short. It passed by so quickly that it took me a while to register what was happening.

"Do you have a portfolio?" the woman asked. She was in charge of setting up the classes with the models, and she was a lot nicer than I expected her to be.

"Uh, no. I never modeled before." I was ready for the death blow.

"Well, that's alright, you can send in your resume and I'll look it over right now."

"Um… sure, I can do that. I'll do that right now." I had no idea what was going on anymore, but I still managed to get her email address in my mounting confusion. Twenty minutes after I sent in my resume, she called me back. I got the job.

Aside from Erick, I didn't tell that many people about the particulars of the new gig. My mother didn't like the sound of me standing naked in a room surrounded by complete strangers. My father didn't protest as much.

"You're an adult," he said when I told him. "I can't make your decisions for you." Whether he was comfortable with the fact, he never did say. But he had my back and that was all that mattered to me.

I only told a few people at church. Their reactions told me enough to keep that information to myself; they meant well, but for them I might have told them that I was a prostitute.

"Are you still going to do that nude thing?" one of them asked me after service one day. I already knew that she wasn't all that crazy about it, but I really didn't care.

"I have my first class next week," I said with a smile.

She frowned. "I really think you should quit." This wasn't the first time that she expressed this sentiment to me. I just shrugged off the comment. There was really nothing else to say about the matter, and I might as well let her go on about something that I already made up my mind about.

I didn't immediately start working as I had hoped to; another two months passed before they called me. Since I came in so late in the school year, there was a chance I wouldn't get any work. Finally, I got a call to come in on the final day. I was terrified. I didn't know what I was getting into. I don't know anything about modeling. I don't know anything about posing. And there was no way in hell I could pull this off, not when I've been gaining weight like it was water. I began imagining scenarios of what would happen if I messed up in any way. It was like I was coming up with ways to talk myself out of it.

I was so nervous that I arrived an hour early. I was even more relieved when I met with the professor a few minutes before class. She was soft spoken and laid-back; in my anxious state, I was expecting some stern, snobbish type.

"You're going to be a dead person for us today," she said cheerfully while pointing at the platform she had set up for me. The thin mattress was placed right in the middle of the room and was bordered with small, thick tree branches. Playing dead sounded doable. It was beginning to look like this day will go better than I thought.

For the next three hours, I laid unmoving on the mattress under a bright spotlight. I was so preoccupied with keeping still that I forgot about the twelve people circled around me. For the first time in my life, I was glad that I didn't have my glasses on. I picked a spot on the ceiling and stared off into the distance.

There were some moments when I spaced out completely. I didn't pass out or anything of the sort; I simply entered this level of peace that I could never find on my own—I was always too fidgety to do such a thing. I did nearly pass out halfway through the class. Apparently, lying on your back for too long can make you lightheaded. The professor kept urging me to take a break, but I was too nervous to do so. One can say that I was trying very hard to make a first impression.

By the time I was finished, my lips were glued shut from my spit and my back ached as I sat up. As I put my robe on, I caught a glimpse of one student's drawing. I squinted towards it, and I saw a beautiful charcoal drawing of my body, surrounded by the small branches placed around my mattress. I was peaceful and glowing, the exact opposite of how I saw myself. I quickly looked away, trying very hard not to blush.

The professor came up to me after I stepped off the platform. "You did a great job," she said. A wave of relief washed over me for the first time in weeks. *I did great.* I could do nothing but smile all the way home after that.

144

I still model from time to time. I've become more comfortable with every class. I still get nervous from time to time, still feel the nakedness of my skin against the glare of the fluorescent lights, but then I see myself on paper, draped in charcoal like some celestial figure, and I know I've made the right choice.

WHAT WE'RE CAPABLE OF: A REJOICE
Emily Blair

We are capable of running free through the tall grasses in the field out back.

We are capable of learning to surf on the Pacific Ocean.

We are capable of building a birdhouse together and watching the birds come visit.

We are capable of learning the symbolic art of karate.

We are capable of breaking a block of wood with our hands.

We are capable of throwing a Frisbee across the lawn to our friend.

We are capable of jumping periodically as the jump rope skims the ground beneath our feet.

We are capable of pushing our little cousin on the swing.

We are capable of swinging alongside our cousin, pumping our legs back and forth, back and forth.

We are capable of climbing a mountain to the very tip top and looking out over the vastness of the world.

We are capable of descending beneath the sea and observing another world.

We are capable of playing a melody across the piano that leaves us with a song stuck in our head.

We are capable of doing a cartwheel in the middle of the parking lot just because we feel like it.

We are capable of riding a horse bareback across the open lands of Montana.

We are capable of executing a perfect cannonball into the deep end of our neighborhood pool.

We are capable of taking our dog for a walk alongside the creek on a warm afternoon.

We are capable of swinging across the monkey bars, maybe even reaching for every other if we're feeling bold.

We are capable of plucking flowers out of the field and pinning them into our hair.

We are capable of climbing a tree, branch by branch by branch.

We are capable of running fast enough to catch the lightning bug we saw across the lawn.

We are capable of reaching high enough to get the sugar off the top shelf.

We are capable of dancing alongside our friends at homecoming to our favorite song that just came on.

We are capable of falling down and scraping our knee.

We are capable of getting back up.

We are capable of balancing on our tip toes as we twirl across a stage.

We are capable of bowing in front of an audience after our performance.

We are capable of pedaling down the rocky path as we go exploring with our friends.

We are capable of moving the log that it is in our path so we can get through.

We are capable of collecting seashells along the shore to take home with us as a souvenir.

We are capable of building a tall and intricate sandcastle.

We are capable of lying on the ground to look at the stars in the sky.

We are capable of filling our lungs with air as we hold our breath in awe.

Darling, we are capable of all of these things, yet you're afraid of me. *Don't be afraid anymore.*

TAKING BACK BEAUTY

Lilian Bustle

I refer to myself as beautiful. And because of that, I hear this a lot: *You can call yourself whatever you want, but beauty is in the eye of the beholder!*

Is it, though? I guess it can be, but that definition of beauty only covers attraction or aesthetic preference. That definition of "beauty" refers to resale value, not inherent value. See, my opinion of something or someone doesn't take away from its inherent value. Yes, I think I'm pretty, but when I talk about beauty, I'm not talking about curb appeal.

Your feelings about the way something looks don't change its beauty. It just means that you don't want to eat it, or live in it, or wear it. Just because you don't like a person's voice or body, or you don't want to have sex with that person, that doesn't take away from that person's value. You could walk into the Sistine Chapel and say "What a dump!" but that doesn't make it less beautiful.

I don't remember exactly when I realized that I was fat, but it was pretty early in life. My older sister was naturally thin, and folks would criticize my Mom saying she didn't feed her enough, so maybe my Mom saw that as a competition she could "win" by feeding me. Later in life I found out that my Mom had been sexually abused by her father. People who have been abused like this often gain weight, sometimes as a grab for protection from a repeat offense, and I often wondered if my Mom wasn't fattening me up as a pre-emptive strike. But that's ridiculous, of course. Being fat doesn't protect you from sexual assault.

I do remember when I first learned that fat people should be hated. In first grade, kids were calling me fat and being mean to me. When I told my teacher, I had hoped she would take the mean kids aside and have a chat with them. Instead, she announced to the class

149

that I *wasn't* fat, but that I was just more to love. It sounded like a nice thing to say, but right away I was horrified. First of all, I *was* fat, and it made me upset that she said I wasn't; and secondly, I knew immediately that she had painted a target on my back. After that, I was officially a pariah at school.

As I grew older, I found friends and solace in the drama department at school and in community theater. The first time I set foot on a stage, I knew that I wanted to perform. I loved to sing and act, but it wasn't long before I realized that because of my size I would never be considered an ingénue. I played Grandma, maid, best friend, turtle, a middle-aged stroke victim, a character actually named Fatty Pert, and The Widow in Taming of the Shrew, all before the age of 21. I got really good at age makeup. In college, when I played Lady Bracknell in *The Importance of Being Earnest*, I thought that's it, I've peaked! That's the best role I'll ever get to play. Even worse was the realization that after college, in the real world, I wasn't even going to get cast in those older roles because there are, um, actual older actors to play them.

Theater and film have no room for fat girls in their twenties, and I didn't have the gumption or money to produce my own show. Crappy survival jobs were essential, so I'd have a flexible schedule to go to auditions, and I went to a lot of auditions. I earned my Actor's Equity Association card and joined SAG/AFTRA, which meant I could audition for Broadway and other paying acting jobs and be considered for better TV and film roles. Hurray! Then I spent more years auditioning and not getting anywhere. Finally, I gave up my Equity card and accepted that I was probably not going to be a working actor.

Then, within five years, all of this happened: my Dad died, then my Grandma died, then I married the wonderful man I'd been dating for years, and 364 days before our one-year wedding anniversary, my Mom died too. My husband and I went through hell mourning and settling their affairs and found a great therapist. Then I took a class at the New York School of Burlesque, and I fell in love with performing again.

I found it. I found the medium that I could use to create my own

150

art, without waiting for someone else's permission. I found stages that welcomed my body and my creativity, and audiences that went wild when I performed. And I reconnected with my beauty. At first, my husband was a little mystified that I wanted to take my clothes off onstage, but he was always supportive, and now he's my biggest fan. Five years later I'm producing my own shows, teaching classes, and performing in international festivals. A couple of years ago I did my TEDx talk, *Stripping Away Negative Body Image*, which addresses Burlesque and body politics. I gave the presentation live for an audience of about 100 people, and I felt really good about it afterwards! I thought *oh maybe I shifted a few paradigms, I'm glad I did this.* But when the video of my talk was posted online, I was totally blown away by the positive response. People are ready to talk about body image and harassment and are ready to reject body shame. It's happening right now, and it's thrilling. Change is in the air.

The world of Burlesque isn't a utopia or a safe haven. It's competitive, and there are plenty of producers who still think that audiences only want to spend money to see thin, white, female bodies. But there are lots of shows that celebrate body diversity, and Queerness, and gender nonconforming people, and those shows make my heart sing. If my body could talk, it would say *SHOW ME TO PEOPLE! Show them you're proud of me, show them how beautiful we are, show them they don't have to prefer a body type to show respect to the person in that body! Show them all.*

Burlesque isn't for everyone, and that's ok. Neither is body positivity, quite frankly. You can stop hating your body and find empowerment without actively celebrating your body. You can also celebrate your body and find great joy in it without taking your clothes off. Burlesque was my paradigm shift, but you can find what's right for you, and find a place of acceptance and love without adhering to anyone else's standards. We have a lot of fighting left to do to change the minds of the many people who would prefer that we stay quiet and apologize for our bodies until we make ourselves as small as possible, but while we're fighting, we can lift each other up and remind each other we're not alone. We are all so beautiful, and we deserve to claim that word.

MY BODY IN FINE PRINT
Aimee Herman

My body [1]

     is fine [2]

          d. [3]

               (no, I haven't) [4]

---

[1] All these ladders exist to reach the heights that ligament-stretch cannot. I went to fourteen different hardware stores to find a ladder, which could reach the angles of my body that I have difficulty talking about. Difficulty reaching. The thing is, no one ever prepares you how to remain in your body after a B&E (breaking and enter). There is no such thing as a box full of all the texts and weaponry to get you through to get you through. Like when I was fifteen and a half and my uterus decided to open up like an apple ripped apart with unapologetic teeth, but instead of hard seeds, there was just lots and lots of blood. My mother gave me a cardboard box with everything she thought I needed to get through to get through. I bring the only ladder I own, which was also given to me by my mother when I moved for the sixth time or the third time. Just a step ladder, but enough to make a difference, so I brought it with me on date number one with human number six so they could view the fine print on my body that my teeth and chin could not pronounce. This human told me they'd rather hear the stories. They wanted me to read them the love story between when we met (um, hospital in New Jersey, after the screams of my mother and the rub of her fluids de-blurred my flesh). And the moment I fell for it. Fell for what? I ask. "For your body. Like truly realized the awe and poetry of it." I wrap myself in girdles made from scar tissue and fossilized welcome mats. The fine print is please don't touch me there. And also not there. And then, would you mind kissing me from a

153

different room? Just stretch your tongue, use pliers or transplant of some sort. Because. I can't feel you next to me. Otherwise. Otherwise. Collapse.

[2] All I can tell you is that my back was always off limits, except that one time.

[3] At least he took his spandex off first. Scent of bike wheels and mother-trauma. Everyone travels to Colorado for the mountaintops and accessible kale and you know it's one of the skinniest cities in the country. But I wasn't thinking about any of this when he flipped me over and suddenly my back became nothing more than skinned animal hide hiding hiding hiding from the rip apart of the rest of me.

[4] So this is why it might be difficult to harmonize why I shake when men are near me. And this is why my identity is far more attached to tree bark because trees root and shade, rather than steal and remove. And if I had to draw you the shape of my body, it would be dots. Like pixels. Or Rorschach. Or chalk outline like that time you were walking your dog and found yourself inside the body of what once was a body, now just a marker of dust to decide its last moments.

FRECKLES ON THE BUTT
Katie McBroom

Even when others thought there were too many inches surrounding my frame; even when outside voices whispered *there are too many inches, you're not the standard, you are not —*

You're beautiful. You're wonderful.
I'm sorry for not defending you.
I'm sorry for starving you of love and food.

I'm looking back on the words I never said like *love*, the one word I should've fed you more of, the word that should've came naturally to me to say, to love. All of those times I stared at you in the mirror, laughing at you, yelling at those inches before bursting into tears.

You didn't deserve anger.
Today I stop. I make a promise.
I will shower you with love and celebrate your curves, marks, bumps, and bruises.
I will treat you to #SelfCareSunday and spa days and shopping trips.
I will let you wear tight dresses and short shorts.
I will swim naked in the sea.
I will nurture you with chocolate and massages.
I will feed you with the word *love*.
Today I love the love the stretch marks on your thighs, your love handles, and imperfect arms.

I love your long, beautiful breasts, freckles on the butt, and all the tiny scars.

TO THE GIRL WHOSE SOUL I CARRY
Morgan Blair

Don't you know that when I wake you early before the sun that it's because I want your soul to be the first thing to touch this day? I don't whisper a breath of lucidness to drag you maliciously out of sleep. I call you up because in those hours of darkness I have missed your colorful company.

To the girl whose soul I carry:

Don't you know that when you peer at my reflection and you scoff out words of hate, that it hurts me deep inside to know you aren't satisfied with this case? Disgusting, fat, gross, too much, each comment is a drop of fire upon my skin. I wake you early with hopeful spirits, that today the dialogue would shift and for once you might wish to be friends.

To the girl whose soul I carry:

Don't you know that when I grumble I am not trying to cause you harm? I just need some fuel to keep on going to make it through the day. Why do you punch and scream and yell? I promise I am not asking for anything beyond my fill. I won't steer you wrong. Trust me I know what we need. Some of this, some of that, but you have to learn to trust me.

To the girl whose soul I carry:

Don't you know that when I paint it isn't my hands that make the work, but your soul that bleeds onto the page? I love those moments of creating because for once we work together. Your soul warms my tired limbs and allows paint to leak freely out of them. A team creating something the world can see and hold. A visual description of your red spirit which you thought you must withhold.

To the girl whose soul I carry:

Don't you know that I won't leave, that without me your spirit would extinguish, that your presence would cease to be? I don't say that to make you notice. I understand if you forever turn away. This house I've built has been through hell. I am broken, scared, and used. But, I want you to remember that if you keep trying to make me fade, that your spirit too will run dry and your light will become a memory. We are the same. We make up one being. I'm your gateway, your shell, your home. So look me in the eyes when you whisper words of hate and remember I am you. Forever fused is our eternal fate.

Girl whose soul I carry, when I wake you tomorrow at dawn will you give me another chance to show you I am worth getting to know?

AM I MY BODY OR IS MY BODY ME?

Katie Grudens

I don't know. Does anybody know? I just graduated college a month ago and all people can ask me now is "where are you working?" and I simply answer with my silence. Is it not enough to just work on myself?

I am a boat made of bones and skin, fighting against the current, floating on the waves, the ocean beautiful and frightening.

I am a blade of grass, growing with the blend of light and air, swaying on my own, surrounded by many like me.

I am a pulsing heart.

I am inflating lungs.

I am human.

Maybe I am my body *and* my body is me. We both change every day, every month, every year. Every. Breath.

I am not the same person that I will be.

I am not the same person that I was.

When I was 14 years old, a boy told me that I made him want to kill himself. His name was Robby, and he wanted me in the palm of his hands. He was two years older than me and wanted more from my body than my fingers braided with his in the school cafeteria. I held my body back from him and he shot words at me like bullets. I can still feel the dents they made. Or maybe those were just the dents of a razor in my skin. The one I kept under my pillow at night. The one Robby never knew about. The one that left blood on my bracelets and tears on my sheets. I can still feel the dents.

When I was 16 years old, I got my period. I felt my body changing and I felt large. I felt like everyone could tell now that I was a woman and that they were all staring. Eyes burned me in the hallway and my own eyes burned me in the mirror. I wanted nothing more than to swallow a knife whole and feel it scrape my throat, drop into my stomach, sink into my skin and rip me open. I wanted red to fill my mouth, to soak my gums, to seep in my pores, to spill on the ground. I wanted death. Or at least a hole in my stomach. I had hoped that maybe with a hole there, the food I ate would fall right out and I wouldn't gain weight. But this was just a hope. Instead, I decided to eat the same amount as my identical twin sister so that we could stay the same weight. I counted each chip she brought to her mouth, fourteen. The sips of milk in the morning before church, six. The pieces of pasta that were dry and the pieces of pasta covered in sauce, twelve, nineteen. I counted everything while my body, now a woman and not a child, became smaller and smaller.

When I was 18 years old, I had my first kiss. His name was Mitch and we were sitting drunk, on a bus, after prom was boring and we all left early. Cheap vodka sat on my lips and we were headed to the city. Speakers were propped up behind us blaring rap music and other kids were making out across from us, giving each other lap dances in suits and ball gowns. I wanted that. I wanted to feel someone against me like that, for someone to tell me I was beautiful, for the hunger of my body to finally end. I stared at those kids with glazed eyes and Mitch grabbed my cheek. His lips tasted like vodka too and I didn't know if I was kissing right but that's okay. I grabbed the back of his head and let my tongue feel his. I closed my eyes and felt his breath blend with mine.

When I was 18 years old, later that same year, I went to college and had my first boyfriend. His name was Conner and I fell in love with his stained glass eyes the moment I saw them. We talked about sex once, sitting in the lounge of the dorm, and I admitted I was a virgin. He said he wasn't and I got nervous. Would he still like me? Another night I went to his room to watch a movie and he slipped his fingers down my shorts and into me. It felt so good but I was confused. I felt drunk again but no vodka sat on my lips this time and I didn't know if my body was normal or what he was thinking. Was this how it was supposed to feel? Did I feel like other girls he has been with? Does he like this? Do I? I told him that I had to go and I wasn't that type of girl. He texted me later that night and said he was sorry. I wanted him to touch me again. Soon after he broke up with me and most of me knows that it was because I wasn't ready for more yet. He, too, wanted more than just my fingers braided with his.

When I was 21, after making out with over fifty boys, I lost my virginity to a boy named PJ. It was my senior year and this boy really liked me and I wanted to get it over with. It hurt and it was awkward and we stopped. But soon, we kept going. This was what people wrote songs about, what people wrote books about, what Robby wanted, what Mitch wanted, what Connor wanted. Now what PJ wanted. Now what I wanted. Soon we were making love all the time, everywhere. He saw me naked, raw, pure, and he still wanted me. He told me I was beautiful. He told me that he loved me. He said that he loves my body and my mind. He told me I am more than just my body.

I know I am.

MELT

Jim Warner

It's not the color of my skin, it's the volume. Even though I've begun to vanish, each stretch mark distends. Tent pole rib cage collapses the tan canvas; folds of flesh deflate. In bed I feel the fat melt only enough to reduce down to an adipose pig pile.

    muscle
    memory pine
    needles
    blanket the
    forest floor

Sexual dysfunction bathes in streetlight. Lungs are full of fiberglass and fluid. She has to be on top but it's her shame, which covers both of us. No one comes. She gets engaged a year later to a graphic designer with a rounder belly. She smiles slightly in a photo. Her bedroom smelled like Starbucks. It's the only thing I'll remember about her taste.

    apple pie
    fold the
    matchbook
    over her
    name

Resting heart rate under 60. Poured heart from a gelatin mold. 115 pounds lighter and I'm more afraid to be naked.

MIND: BODY–A FRAGMENTED SOLILOQUY
Dawn Leas

Tell

I've always been slightly afraid of you and your potential. This fear sprouted early in childhood when I overheard hushed conversations of adults, and then when I was older, I was brought into the circle of discussions—a heart that stopped at 25; the pain of gnarled rheumatoid arthritis fingers; managing low potassium levels with medicine the color of Tang; how cells can go rogue for years until a tumor the size of a grapefruit is found; an aneurysm explodes in belly or brain; undiagnosed stomach cancer that spreads its tentacles. If these ailments struck family members, surely you could use that DNA against me.

Then, there was your dark side, your want—for lust, love, food, attention—that bloomed, blossomed and ballooned. Early on, I seemed to know they were something to hide; to apologize for. I felt that curiosity deep in my earliest memories, maybe age three? I woke from a nap and in the haze of half-sleep felt the tingle of physical pleasure. It was almost orgasmic. I have buried that primal pull toward physical desire, but throughout the years, you left it on a slow simmer just beneath the surface of the skin. You didn't want to be tamed.

Silence

Willow Avenue. Mom and Dad had turned the spare bedroom into a den with an orange 70's carpet and a console TV. On the weekends, we would watch *Wild Kingdom* and eat tuna sandwiches on Wonder Bread. At night it was *Zoom* while Mom fried chicken in the kitchen down the hall, the sizzle audible and the oil smell rumbling our stomach.

This is where an older neighborhood boy got down on the floor with us. He tented a blanket over your legs. He pulled down your pants, parted your legs, and touched you. His fingers prodded, pushed open and moved in. I turned to the TV and watched the images flicker across the screen. I was silent. Of course, he told me it was just like going to the doctor. I knew how to keep secrets, and I did. Of course, I told no one until I was older, and as each person dismissed it—ex-boyfriend, husband, nurse, therapist—I took on waves of more shame and believed that you wanted it, attracted it, made it happen.

Murmur

New Orleans. We lived on one side of a duplex that was icy when the temperature dropped close to 30 in February. We listened to Carol King's *Tapestry*. We played marathon games of Life in the closet under the stairs with cousins visiting from the north. You cracked open crabs, and I was afraid of the dead man's fingers inside. You were allowed to have plenty of Twinkies and Kool Aid, but I craved the cottage cheese the Tulane student who babysat us ate for dinner.

We rode a streetcar along St. Charles Avenue to the French Quarter with Mom, Grandma and Great-Grandma. You ate beignets, the powder sugar falling onto your halter-top. You drank cold milk. We walked Bourbon Street with Mom trying to cover your eyes. You strained to see into the darkened doorways, hear the music and conversation inside the bars and clubs. I knew something was going on in there that might be forbidden. *You* wanted to know the details.

The bathroom had powder blue tile. One day, while toweling dry after a shower, I caught a glimpse of your stomach. It protruded slightly. I remembered advertisements and television shows of how a girl's body should look. I willed you to make a fist. You punched your belly. I felt rage. We were in second grade.

Hum

Texas. We lived in Denton during a record-setting heat wave and drought. Temperatures above 100 and no rain. Cracks opened, looked like veins crisscrossing scorched fields. Mom's goldfish died, nearly boiled to death. We sunned your skin to a deep brown. You ate salads because you loved iceberg lettuce when others ate ice cream. You drank sweetened tea and Coke.

We went to high-school football games, and I dreamed of being a cheerleader. I wanted to be older; you wanted to be freer. I argued with Mom about shaving your legs. She acquiesced, but only to right above the knee. She took us shopping for your first bra. I wasn't happy about the size we bought. I wanted you to bleed so I could join the club our older cousins and twin sister already had memberships in. I wanted to pass this rite. I thought you were holding back on purpose, to tease me. You seemed to want to take your time getting there.

I realized that there was a physical reaction to boys, that the heart picked up its pace and the mouth dried when Mark with his Texan drawl skated around the rink in Wranglers and an Oxford shirt. The butterflies fluttered at the sight of his freckled face and chocolate brown hair. The knot in the stomach tightened when he skated away. You wanted to be kissed. But I said good girls don't do that.

Roar

Pennsylvania. We were the new girl with braces and big glasses with our initials in the lower corner of the left lens. I talked funny. I didn't fit in. Your hair only feathered like Farrah's on one side. The other was listless, untrainable. I wanted to morph into an Izod-wearing preppy whose family had lived in one area for four generations. Boys chased you on the playground trying to goose you. I wanted to be the teacher's pet. You rolled our school uniform above the knee. We were pulled out of class by another teacher to ask if we wanted to switch buses for the trip to the Franklin Institute. I knew plans were being made for kissing in the back seat as the bus sped through the Lehigh Valley Tunnel. Timmy stood behind the teacher hands in prayer position begging me to say yes. I wanted to be invisible. You wanted to be touched. I said no.

You roared throughout high school. I spent late-nights with best friends talking about sex. You craved Kraft Mac & Cheese and mashed

165

potatoes. I fell in love. He taught you things we had only heard about or seen in the movies. Other guys paid attention to you. Our first love was jealous. We met an older guy who worked in a drug store on the weekends. You liked him. He said we were too young. I waited to get older so we could go out with the older guy.

I struggled to maintain a good-girl image. You were busy urging our first love's hand and tongue to wander the curves of you, to find the spots that always took you to another world. I was ashamed of your wanting this.

Break Silence

Into adulthood, I played the "if only" game—if only you lost 10 pounds; if only you had thicker hair; if only you didn't have stretch marks across our stomach and breasts; if only you didn't love chocolate and mashed potatoes and pasta thick with parmesan cheese and olive oil; if only you stuck to an exercise routine; if only you didn't want so much—we would be healthier, fitter, stronger, happier. You and I could get along. We would be whole.

I felt defined by that neighborhood boy. You carried the weight of shame. I carried the weight of guilt. I wanted to run from sex. You fanned lustful fires. I wanted to be the perfect wife. You grew restless. I had to prove that you could fight against urges. You sought adventure. I failed miserably at most of this. You want to open me to possibility.

Voice

I used to be ashamed of your weaknesses—middle-of-the-night leg pain, which Mom always called "growing pains." Sharp, electric pinch in thumb and wrist from overuse. Sore shoulder from twisting the wrong way taking off t-shirt. The white-fog of an ailing thyroid, a plummeting Vitamin D level. The paralyzing concrete of depression. The shrieking siren of cluster migraines. Hip pain that caused you to rise slowly from sitting crossed-legged on the floor.

I am done ignoring that communication from you. Now, I am in awe of those messages. I see them as beacons—signs that things weren't quite right and that we needed a perspective change, an attitude adjustment, to get still and quiet together, to get unstuck.

I have always and still do respect your strength. Training for softball and basketball in middle-school kept you conditioned. In our early 20s, you carried two babies and pushed them into the world. Your sexy legs were built by years of lifting and spinning and walking and running. Your arms sculpted by push-ups done on the bedroom floor and while doing yoga videos late at night. The physical movement you used to pull me out of the setting concrete to help me walk away, to move ahead.

Echo

I mediate a lot these days on letting go. I imagine constructing a paper boat (not sure how well that would work in reality) and piling it high with old tapes, memories, and emotions, pushing it into a river and watching it float closer to, and eventually over, the waterfall.

In reality, we are not drawn to rivers but to salt water. Last summer as a storm was forming, we ran away to the cobalt Cape Cod Atlantic. It was chilly, so we swam in a bay warm as bathwater. A steady wind churned its surface, filled our ears. We let it buoy us, let it carry us away and for that 15-minute swim the outside world didn't exist. It was just you and me. We were in the eye of the storm. I heard our breath. I felt our heart beating. My thoughts and your want echoed each other.

At that time, we knew choppy waters were ahead of us. The storm raged. We held on. A year later, the clouds are clearing. We can see the horizon. I feel less cluttered. I am shedding old ideas. You seem more at ease with less shoulder pain, the ache of hip fading slowly like a summer day into night. I am speaking up. You are free. We are whole.

ON LOVING A MAGIC BODY
Sarah Bregel

My baby whacks my saggy, half-floating breast in the bathtub and says "boo-boo." He rubs my belly with soap and says "bell-bell." He plays with a tiny plastic walrus toy, lays it on my thigh and says "rawrrrrr" because I didn't know what a walrus said so that's what I told him.

We soak and I explain, in toddler terms, how he and his sister drank from my breast and grew in my belly. "Bodies are strange," his eyes tell me, and mine agree. They are the food we eat, the babies we carried, and nursed. They are the cigarettes we smoked and the vodka we drank in alleys and parking lots and playgrounds when we were fifteen, straight out of the pint that we bought for five dollars, because it's all the money we had from babysitting or mowing an old-lady's lawn. But it didn't matter because it got the job done. They are the cancers we might get from genes or parabens and the anxiety in our shoulders and our chewed up fingernails. They are the too much wine in the evenings and tired mornings and miles we plodded on the treadmill while watching *Love it or List it*.

I look at my body, under this soapy water and I ask myself if everything I'm doing in this life is enough. No—not to fit into my jeans but maybe enough to not get cancer or cirrhosis. Maybe enough that my daughter will like me, love me, come to me and let me listen when she talks. I hope I don't forget how to listen in close. To her, and to everything else that whispers, or screams, begging one way or another, for me to hear it.

When I was a child, my mother went for long runs each day without fail, even when it snowed. She was a size 6, 125 pounds and never more. If she gained a pound or two, she would stand in front of the mirror, waving her belly at me, talking loud and desperately about the terrible, sickening sack of flesh. The way her voice rose when she spoke the words made me want to hide under the bed. Then she'd count calories until the pound or two was gone.

By the time I was 12, I was her same weight and height. But even as a fit adolescent, who played sports and ran faster than all the boys, my body always felt like a work in progress. I couldn't escape that I'd developed quicker than all the other girls. I began to despise my breasts and hips and how in my mind, my womanly figure made me look huge all over. Before long, I was bigger than my own mother. Just five or ten pounds. But I knew it and I knew she knew it, too. And then every time she lifted her shirt and waved her flesh at me, I wondered *if she hates her own body so much, what must she think of mine?*

By eighth grade, my body and I were at odds. One evening my mother took me bathing suit shopping at the local mall before the end of the year pool party. At first I was excited. I would find the perfect suit that disguised all my insecurities- I would look amazing in that suit. I would suck in my gut, like she had always instructed me to do, and no one would know what was underneath.

I settled on a purple and gold tankini, after hours of trying on material that my white belly spilled out of. Finally, I emerged, defeated, from the dressing room, handed it to my mother and told her to buy it. Hot tears of shame streamed down my face as we stood in line. Over and over, she asked me what was wrong, until I stormed out of the store and sat on the sticky floor of the mall with my head in my hands.

When they day of the pool party came, I kept my shorts on all day and sat, glued to a bench. I watched other girls run freely in their bodies. They laughed when boys tackled them and pushed them into the water. I couldn't move an inch.

I didn't feel my daughter being born. In a hospital bed, one I'd been forced into, I labored on my back for hours, begging to be set free. Finally, in the early hours of the morning, drugged and sliced from underneath, a doctor lifted her up, tiny and pink. I was told that at just a shade over five pounds her head could never have fit without the doctor's knife to widen the opening. While he stitched it back up, as quickly as his hands would move, I winced and tried to focus on my baby who was being cleaned and wrapped and weighed.

My body had failed me again, like others had promise it would. Birth was too hard, too terrible to do on your own. Or perhaps I wasn't strong enough to give birth without drugs and tools and machines that beeped.

A few days later, I sat on the edge of my bed, teaching myself to nurse my baby. I posed awkwardly, trying not to disrupt the chain of stitches underneath me while I held my baby to my breast. Suddenly, while my baby sucked on one side, milk poured from the other. It cascaded down my belly and pooled on the bed. I stared at the pale white liquid in disbelief. Magic.

During the first year of motherhood, I got smaller and harder, almost without trying. I wandered the farm road we lived on, overwhelmed and lost in postpartum sadness. My mind was an endless circus of scary, intrusive thoughts, and they were all that I could see. At night my heart beat fast, so fast that I thought it might explode with my own fears. I pressed my fingers to my neck to feel the thumpity-thump and tried to remember breathing.

I walked and jogged, pushing a stroller over dirt roads, yet could scarcely find the time to eat. I wasn't searching for anyone's pre-baby body. I was searching for my childless soul. Instead, I found a shape I'd only ever glimpsed in short spurts- lean and toned and enviable. Still I didn't love it.

The midwives worked quickly and quietly, like tiny mice, filling up the birthing pool which sat on the floor in our basement. For two hours, I swayed and moaned, surrendering to what each wave asked of me gently, then demanded. When I could dance no more, I poured myself into the water which was warmer than I'd expected. It held and comforted me, so I just floated, eyes closed. Waiting.

After one small push, I felt my son's head break through, then his shoulders, and the rest of him. He swam to the surface, reaching his arms to me. I laid him on my chest, our eyes both opened now. His sister came in and rubbed her small hand on the ridges of his skull, then kissed it. She wasn't afraid of him like I thought she might be.

A few weeks after my second child's birth, I sat at the community swimming pool with all of my postpartum flesh just hanging from my bones. I looked nothing like I looked after I had my daughter five years earlier when I was 24 and everything had bounced back and back and back and motherhood had eaten me alive.

With two children who demanded every ounce of me, my body was bigger than it had ever been and it would stay that way for longer than anticipated- my cheeks bloated from lack of sleep, my belly sagging over the lip of my pants, my breasts milk-filled and enormous. Short of running myself ragged, letting my needy infant scream, there was nothing I could do to change it. It was like living in someone else's skin. I wanted to figure out how to introduce myself, to know this version of my body as something worthy. It would've been easier to hate it. But hating it no longer made perfect sense.

I sat next to a mother in a two-piece whose baby was only a little bigger than mine but her belly was tan and hard and flat. I nursed my son while she nursed her daughter and I told myself that nobody really cared about my body except for the one who was drinking from it so that he could fall asleep and get strong. And it wasn't some lie I made up to feel better.

Here in the bath, with my youngest baby babbling and my skin still stretched and soft, my body is enough. And I know that I have never not liked my body. I just didn't understand its magnitude yet. That it could grow two smart, tiny humans and push them out, that it could make milk, or that my heart could beat out of sync with the rest of the world because I was so overwhelmed and my body knew it before I did. But loving your body, or even liking your body takes time and practice and saying "look what I made." And it's just bigger and more important than the shape of what made it.

171

Like my motherhood, my body is loud and upfront. My perpetual truth-teller. It is impossible to run away from. It is all there in the parts that jiggle or have deep stretched out lines across my torso. Or how my daughter really feels about herself, deep down, because of how often I screamed, or spoke quietly and said encouraging words, or made her feel trapped, or was the person for her that I needed once.

It is all there, compiling, or conspiring against me. But my body stayed with me, growing bigger, smaller, then bigger again, and more stretch-marked up. And I had no choice but to befriend it. To know that my body is so many more important things than a number and a size. I don't even know what those numbers and sizes are anymore. Just that they are a part of who I am, but not all of who I am. My heart beats and my legs carry me from place to place and my arms that hold my children are stronger than they've ever been, and so am I.

The walrus is looking at me, saying "rawrrr" because my baby believed me. So I try to say what's true. I will tell my babies that my body is a certain kind of magic. I will let them rub their fingers on my stretch marks and *oooh* and *aaah*. And I will finally understand.

BODY LETTER
Ashley Tipton

I am caught in two different parallel worlds. One world where I know we all deserve clothing that makes us feel sexy, comfortable and sassy. As a "plus-size" designer I am always aware of my body and the bodies of others. I have always been "big" and have spent my life "looking in the mirror" and learning to love my self. This journey has not been easy. I know that I must get to a point of self-acceptance before I can begin to work on what I would like my body/health to look like.

I also know that my body doesn't define who I am, yet is a "machine" that can operate most effectively when I begin to treat it well. As I convey my message of self- acceptance and self-love, I cannot fool myself that "for me" this current body is not operating as it could.

This is my message to myself not my message to those I create for. We must all create our own story and journey. I am here to create clothing while we are on it. My hope for others and myself is that as we journey together we will do so on our terms, on our time, and in whatever way we choose.

POUNDS OF SHAME

Jennifer Morgan

There I was, barely above water, pushing against the current. My gap year turned into four wasted years spent chasing young men who crushed my soul. During that time, some of my friends had children and decided to marry the men who made their dreams come true. My other friends went to college and were well on their way to graduation. I was green with envy. Their lives, though different, were so desirable. One set, a family. Stability, something to cherish, foster, and grow. The other, a future, interesting people, interesting places, experiences that do not compare to my nights spent dancing to local bands at local bars. I didn't have someone to impregnate me. No one ever stuck around long enough. I had one choice, I was enrolling in college. I'm moving away and my life is going to be desirable. I finally went to college. I lasted for one whole, yet half-hearted semester.

What card had I drawn in the game of missed chances? My best friend moved 1200 miles away and my married friends were miserably stockpiling diapers. I was convinced that feminists had ruined my life. The same warriors who beat the pavement and never stopped until women could vote, go to college, or get a full-time job. I looked upon these women with contempt. I was imprisoned by the ideals set forth by them. There I sat, 24 years old, with a part-time job as a telephone operator. I was sad, lonely, and quickly losing faith in my ability to forage the life that I had once envisioned. Then, in an instant, my hope was restored. I accepted a dream job offered to me by my best friend's future mother-in-law. I was going to change. I was going to be better. It was all going to turn out *okay*.

Patricia wanted to show me the ropes, expose me to the lucrative underbelly of car insurance and homeowner's policies. By the terms of anything I knew in my 24 years, she was rich. New cars, flashy jewelry, fancy restaurants, expensive handbags, and intellectual friends. Patricia had life experience. She lived in Philadelphia before settling down in the country with her husband where she quickly became a big fish in a small pond. She birthed three children, a marriage, and a business. She had it all, until she watched her children move away and her husband into the arms of another woman. She had a hole in her life and was looking for two things: a man and a project. I quickly discovered I was the latter.

My first few trips into the office beneath Nicholson Train Bridge were filled with excitement. I would learn this business and get rich. I was on the fast track to success. I might even meet a man! However, as the days dragged by, and the crop of local men did not prove bountiful, I didn't feel successful. I wasn't learning much, as Patricia kept me busy running errands for her children, going to the post office, and picking up her lunch on my own dime. I sat in a dusty old office in a town even more Podunk than Scranton. I was a secretary. I was an assistant. I was a protégé. I was a nickname I despised.

One of the most valuable lessons I learned while hatefully smoking cigarettes at the desk across from Patricia, was, that as a fifty-something "rich" divorcee, her life wasn't much better than mine. She desperately wanted the love of a man. She had everything else, yet was not complete because a man did not choose her. She had just returned from Puerto Rico with her boyfriend du jour and it was officially over. He's never leaving his wife. All of her money and accomplishments did not amount to a hill of beans. She had nobody to love.

Dating services, blind dates, reigniting old flames, nothing worked for her. These channels were far too risky for me. I was always the chunky friend. Probably what the kids today refer to as "The Duff." I recall a night out with my best friend, Jennie (beautiful, thin, with long dark hair, an adventure in human form), before she moved away. We met up with two guys we knew at a local bar. They worked in the warehouse at Sears, a place where Jennie and I hustled hand tools on commission for a few years. We had some drinks and once the band started, the guys wanted to dance. I had a huge crush on Danny. I

175

couldn't talk to him without turning red, forget about what would happen on the dance floor, so I decided not to dance. Jennie followed my lead and decided to stay at the table to slam a few more shots. As we walked away at the end of the night, I heard Danny say to his friend "the big one didn't want to dance." *Ouch.* He didn't even refer to me by name. I was "the big one" and most likely not a big enough catch for him. I must have been a lucky big girl though. I must not have been too much of a land monster, as over the course of a few years I found a handful of men to fuck me. Big girls had big tits. Some men settled for that. I settled for that.

One day, Patricia arrived late to the office as she did every morning. Her customers demanded her, and stubbornly, they stood at the counter waiting. I sat awkwardly with watchful eyes on me until she graced us with her presence. She'd hang her coat, put her purse on her desk, light a cigarette, and get started. She was great with them and they ate her up. She made them feel like they were the most important person in the world. She needed them. She needed to fill a void and they poured into her like cement into sidewalk forms. When the lobby cleared, I recognized judgment in her face as she scanned my Fashion Bug business suit from top to bottom. She stopped on my hair. "Jen," she asked, "did you roll out of bed like that today? Your hair looks wild." Note to self: hide naturally curly hair. Stay on course with straight hair, curl flip at the bottom. Check.

As I recovered from the visual assault, Patricia said she had a surprise for me. She signed us up for swing dance lessons at a popular area night club. It was the "in" thing. The Squirrel Nut Zippers, The Stray Cats, and The Brian Setzer Orchestra were making a comeback and everyone needed to hammer down the moves. It was post-war romanticism set to big band music in the late 90s. This was our chance. Dancing. With men. In a club. With drinks. Happiness and acceptance was on the horizon. So off we went, me clunking along in stacked Mary Janes, a long gray skirt and a light blue sweater set, Patricia in her black heels, pencil skirt, and signature Chanel blazer. A veritable odd couple we were, the pauper and the polished.

176

To say it was a bust would be an understatement. Established couples, single mustachioed men, and a few randomly placed single women hugged every wall. We ditched the lessons and headed to the bar. While I was in the restroom, Patricia found me a suitor. Kevin was in finance, 29 years old, with his own place. He was a prospect. We flirted for hours, intermittently including Patricia in the conversation. It was fun and easy and unexpected. As the night wound down, Kevin asked if he could drive me home. I had one Stoli and soda too many and Patricia's maternal gene was running on overdrive. She insisted on following us to a coffee shop near my parent's house (where I lived) with the intense need to confirm that he was not going to dismember me and scatter my parts about the valley. She planned on treating us to coffee. We didn't want coffee, we wanted to add fire to our spark.

My fifty-something gal pal eventually drove off and Kevin asked if he could come to my house. Ummm, what part of living with my parents didn't he understand? I didn't bring men home in the light of day. I wasn't bringing a man home at 2 am. We took a drive and pulled off the main road into the parking lot of a community center. At this time of night, it was a ghost town. We talked some more. He complimented my conversational skills. He complained about the girls at work. *They don't have anything valuable to say. They're gorgeous but vapid.* I looked out the window and envisioned my full figure being dropped off quickly. Instead, he pulled me in for a kiss. The kiss developed into a heated makeout session. He was into it. I was into it. Had we not been in the front seat of an Acura sports car, the situation would have escalated. Again, he showered me with compliments. I was so passionate, I was a great kisser, I was so pretty.

I was buzzing from a combination of endorphins, vodka, and adoration. Wow. I haven't felt this way in years. It had been, gasp, three years since my last sexual encounter. I needed this lift. We weren't having sex tonight, but it was on the horizon. Kevin turned to me, he held my face in his hands, and said "You have such a beautiful face." I could have died. Validation. Someone thought I was beautiful. Jackpot. If only he stopped there. "If you lost 50 pounds, you would be a total knockout. 50-80 pounds." Well that felt like a ton of bricks.

177

At 178 pounds, I was overweight by most standards, but hardly a heifer. If Kevin's suggestion came to fruition, I would be an emaciated 98 pounds. A gorgeous, vapid, girl. My buzz disappeared and I asked to go home. As I was getting out of the car, we exchanged numbers. Foolishly, I called him the next day. No answer. No answering machine. Needless to say, we never spoke again.

I couldn't get by his evaluation of my worth. What an arbitrary number, 80 pounds. It's almost as if Kevin were a carnival barker and could calculate my weight by sight. Stunned, I found myself in the same place as that night in the bar with Jennie and our two guys: *I was the big one who wouldn't dance.* I was a woman who was not worthy of love, affection, or attention. I spent the next two decades wondering who would love me and for how long, always holding those numbers- Kevin's numbers- 50-80 pounds in my mind.

Looking back now, these preoccupations were never dependent on my weight. They were dependent upon my frame of mind. My fear of being undesirable devoured every ounce of confidence I may have owned. I was consumed by flowing with the current of what is deemed beautiful. The memories of rejection still shine like a fresh coat of paint in my mind. Truth be told, it would take much more than 50-80 pounds to be loved and desired. It would take one thing: *time.* And it has taken nearly all of those eighteen years to realize that love and value is not measured in weight.

SKINNY PERSONALITY
Lis Mesa

My average evening consists of a bottle of cheap wine, a pint of ice cream, and six to seven consecutive hours of Netflix.

This is how I gained 100 pounds over the last five years of my 20s.

The time when I was supposed to be building my career, traveling the world and settling down with *the one*. All my skinny friends were doing it, so I tried to do it too, but nothing I accomplished in this bigger body ever felt like accomplishing anything at all.

I remember sporadic weigh-ins—the numbers on my bathroom scale, that once looked like familiar faces began to turn into strangers. I stared through them as I suddenly jumped from 140 to 170 to 200, 225 and then stopped at 240. I haven't stepped on the scale since.

However, I don't remember the specifics of how the weight came on, there isn't one particularly shocking moment where my body shuddered, sending signals to my mind to do something about it.

Another person would have been alarmed. They would have talked to a physician; a dietician- they would have purchased a gym membership.

I looked at that body every day and didn't realize what was happening. I didn't understand that over the years my *skinny personality*—a defense mechanism that had cemented into my skull, burying itself deep within in order to protect my sentiments—had taken over. This mentality stopped me from recognizing the fact that my body was morphing into something I didn't like, something that made me physically sick, something that kept me from attempting the things in life I most hoped to achieve.

It starts in childhood. I started school in the US at the age of 6. A Cuban immigrant, I had to learn the language, when I did—I spoke it with a heavy accent. I was very shy and very tall and very wide. The other kids avoided me, all I wanted was a friend.

During elementary school, on a bright morning, a confident girl passed around cupcakes on her birthday. As she handed me one, I said "Thank you." She took it back before it reached my hand, saying "Never mind. Not you." I looked around the classroom, everyone had one but me.

In middle school, my mom picked out my clothes. She dressed me in baggy jeans and baggy t-shirts. She didn't buy me a training bra, though I desperately needed one. My hair was thick with oil, though my mom washed it every day. For school, she'd slick it back into a tight ponytail- exposing a large, round face covered in red pimples and wire-rimmed glasses with thick lenses.

I wasn't allowed to shave my legs and armpits, which were covered in coarse dark hair or wear deodorant or body splash to mask the scents my body had begun giving off.

My body was rapidly developing, growing out of my control, but my mom didn't recognize it—she still saw me as a child. She didn't know that in this new country children grew up faster.

I tried to make friends. In a park behind the school, before classes started, I followed a group of kids who liked to share cigarettes and beer before homeroom. They stared as I approached, before one of them picked up a rock and threw it- hitting my shoulder. He picked up another one and shouted, "We don't want you here troll, leave!" He threw the second rock, hitting my leg as the other kids began to shout "Troll, troll..." and others, "Monster, get out of here! Leave!"

I stood there, as each person in the group picked up a rock and threw it. I stood until someone broke my glasses, and made my nose bleed. I didn't cry. A girl spoke up saying that it was enough, they all dropped their rocks and walked away. I sat in the park that entire day until my mom picked me up in the afternoon and I never, ever talked about it again.

180

My parents had escaped communism. Both former University professors and engineers, my mother found work as the only female employee at a car parts factory while my father sold water filters door to door and worked a fruit stand at a local flea market on the weekends. How could I make life harder for them, by letting them share in my shame?

We were a loving family, where my quirks—my stories, my opinions were cherished. My parents had done enough for me by making me believe that my insides were great- but, the outside world had now shown me that my outsides needed a lot of work.

I had to change-on my own—this was not who I wanted to continue being. No one saw me as I saw myself.

I went into high school with a strategy. I got a notebook and on the first page wrote, "My Self-Improvement Plan" and this included losing the weight and the glasses. Changing my hair and how I dressed like. I wanted to be shiny and new and it took me all four years, but I did it. I became that person I had written notebook after notebook about.

I graduated in 2005 in Miami, FL.. That summer before college, I was reborn. I was thin and tan and wore Abercrombie and Fitch mini-skirts and tank tops with Hawaiian prints on them and Pookah shell necklaces and bright pink nail polish to match my bright lipstick. I dyed blonde strips into my hair and got my lip pierced with a silver hoop.

I had become loud and confident and shiny and new.

I started dancing and drinking and kissing in the Midtown warehouses—White Room, The Vagabond, Spider Pussy—before the neighborhood became Wynwood, gentrified, polished, as it stands today, over a decade later.

I danced with all the boys that had never looked at me, I took pride in being able to out-drink them all and still hold it together. I kissed all those boys, maybe 20 of them, maybe a little more. Their names carefully listed in the back page of my notebook, a check mark next to each of their names.

I entered my 20s high—high on this life, on this persona I had managed to create. This "skinny personality" erased every painful memory before then.

At 21, I ran along the Miami Beach sands. My tall body cast a long shadow across the surf. In the ocean, my long, dark hair waved across the water, floated like tentacles on a jelly fish. I was Amazonian, able to survive out in the wild while the canopy of glittering hotels existed in their civilized state behind me.

My "skinny personality" had given me an armor. I could tuck those childhood memories somewhere within it, and show only a steel and leather breast plate to the world. I had learned that if you're big and tall for your age, you do everything in your power to become smaller because you truly believe skinny, little girls can fit in anywhere and they never get hurt. If you're shy and innocent, you become loud and wild because no one would throw rocks at someone who could shout and fight, fiercely, for themselves.

I became unstoppable. Six times per week I met with a personal trainer in the morning. In the afternoons, I'd alternate between running three miles on the treadmill, burning calories in a spin class, or sweating through Hot Yoga.

My menu was limited; my portions were small. I followed strict rules: No sugar. No carbs. No beer or wine. I woke up early, had a protein shake and began my work out, I stuck to my routine.

My "skinny personality" empowered me and created nights where *everything was beautiful and nothing hurt.*

On those nights, I wore little black dresses, drinking double vodka tonics men bought me at every bar I went to.

My friends and I stood in front of bathroom mirrors, crouching over toilet seats, holding each other's drinks, lighting cigarettes we never inhaled. We reapplied our mascara and asked, "Aren't we so special?" "So privileged?" "So lucky to be able to dance the night away while children starved in Africa?" We concluded that we were starving here, so we "kind of" got it and that made it okay.

As those nights turned to years, we started bringing out the blow and shoving eye liner pencils down our throats, watching as chunks flew out of our mouths into every bathroom stall we ever visited.

That time was marked by the mist of a club, the foggy haze of a Sunday hangover.

I don't know how I managed to scamper out of the dark corners of those places. The lights must have come on during last call and I must have scattered away like a fucking roach. All that was left of me by then was a husk—one found by a tall, dark, handsome stranger who didn't quite know what to make of it all.

I didn't tell this man my story, not from the beginning. I led with something I thought was sexy, a number of superficial anecdotes from the 6 months I lived and partied in Brooklyn, which had worked for me so many times with so many men at so many bars.

Mark called me out. Told me that what I've called my "skinny personality" was just a front. All talk, a wall, a barrier. Something that was keeping the good in me inside—hidden, so that all he could see at this moment were all the terrible things I had become.

The night we had this conversation, I threw on a pair of yoga pants and climbed into his bed, where we watched a movie and ate two entire pizzas.

I'd just turned 25 and needed a break. The last few years had been loud—much too fast, yet way too long. I could rest a while. It felt so calm and quiet in his arms.

This is how extremes work.

The noise from the TV startles me awake. Memories from the last few years suddenly rush in, like a 100-pound bag of bricks smashing me hard across the face, and I'm slapped wide awake into the present.

It has been 5 years since that moment in Mark's bed, and I discover I've been out—in a food comma, wasting away on the couch. The chattering coming for the TV screen making me realize I've been distracted, connected to realities that are not quite my own.

Startled, I look around for a reset button that does not exist.

The lights get brighter. This is the third doctor's office I've visited in a week. This is where the terms obesity, Polycystic Ovary Syndrome, high blood pressure, inflammation and pre-diabetes are explained to me, over and over again. This is when I'm terrified.

The lights dim. Now is when I hear through a friend of a close friend that the reason I am not a bridesmaid at the wedding is because I'm too heavy and would throw off the visual aesthetics of the event. This is when my heart breaks.

It is now dark and I can't sleep at night. I break into cold sweats and my heart races and I have to remind myself that I'm not in danger. That this is just the Generalized Anxiety Disorder and the Major Depression I've been diagnosed with, and soon the three different types of meds I've been prescribed should get me through the night.

This is when I realized that the panic button had been in me all along. It'd been there since the day those kids threw those rocks, when I should have pressed it—hard—and screamed for help.

Now, I'm expected to soften the shock on friend's faces who haven't seen me in a while by making jokes about the weight I've gained. I find myself discussing my personal medical history with strangers who offer unrequited weight loss advice, assuring them that I have some control over what is happening inside my body. An older co-worker shows me a photo and says, "Look at how skinny you used to be, you were so pretty." I nod and walk away.

"There's a person in here who is still trying to polish herself shiny and new, every day as she grows," shouts my skinny personality. I don't believe anyone can look past the body and hear *her*.

This whole thing. It's a story. It's a body. But it's not me. I'm still that Amazon on the beach, now just unable to run because I'm dragging 100 pounds—of fear, loss and regret—across the sand, burning my feet, slowly getting closer to the ocean once again.

THIGHS THAT TOUCH

Leah Vernon

"The reason why your aunt can't get a job is because she's fat," Mom said matter-of-factly to my younger sister and me.

In my own fat thirteen-year old body I thought, *that's not the reason why. It's just a bad economy.*

Although Mom wasn't as big as my aunt, her weight was up and down. Mostly up. She had suffered from eating disorders for most of her life, including mild anorexia. To be honest, I never really recalled Mom eating "real food" like the stuff she fed us. She was a closet eater who binged on cakes and doughnuts in the privacy of her bedroom. The sheets would be riddled with crumbs and the aroma of sugary frosting lingered.

Mom showed us old photos of her younger, thinner self in the 70s, wearing short shorts, a crop top, and rocking a thick, black afro. She said proudly while pointing, "See. My thighs didn't touch back then. When they touched, I knew that I was eating too much."

Thin was good in our house. Great even. Fat was unacceptable.

And I was fat.

My thighs touched. My belly hung over my panties. My boobs jumped when I jumped. My double chin greeted you before I was able to. My arms squeezed into jackets that didn't stretch.

Obsession.

One day I decided to turn on my own fat body. To mistreat it like it was my worst enemy. To destroy it until there was nothing left. I was tired of boys only flirting with my thin friends, I was tired of stuffing myself into jeans that only made it partially up my thick thighs, and I was sick and tired of obsessing over how other people perceived my fat ass! *Am I eating too fast? Should I get the salad instead? Should I just shut up? Who wants to hear what a fattie has to say?*

Scouring the latest teen fashion magazines, I ripped out dozens of pages of unrealistic supermodels, thin white actresses, and statuesque bombshells with straight white teeth. I went on a rampage and started pasting them on my bedroom wall, the closet door, and around my dresser's mirror. I wanted to see what I wasn't, but what I could possibly be. Skinny and beautiful. Wanted and validated. Mom would be proud of me. Only if my thighs didn't touch.

I went out and bought a pair of stylish jeans that were two or three sizes too small. When I got home, I placed them on a hanger and hung them on the window over my bed. It was my motivation. The person who could fit inside those jeans was better in some way. Outgoing. A fuckin' boss.

I envisioned myself in those jeans every morning when I woke up before school, when I ate a handful of pretzels and drank a low-calorie drink for lunch, when I thought about having a slice of pizza, and right before I went to bed. My inability to focus and the migraines due to malnutrition didn't matter. Nor had the churning and grinding of my stomach. Not even the silent late night tears due to gaining a half a pound the prior day meant anything.

After five months, I had lost seventy pounds. And how things changed. Everyone was so happy. It was as if I had won some sick lottery. My teachers asked me how I did it. "It's easy," I lied. Guys started to notice me. Girls were jealous of me. I was living the life.

At home, when the cheers died and I was all alone, I was still fat. Inside. The scale said one thing, but my mind told me another.

Losing the weight was brutal. Maintaining it was different. My antics got wilder as I scrambled to stay thin. In the morning, I'd clear my bowels and bladder, strip, and hop on the scale butt naked. If the scale was even a pound heavier, my entire day would be ruined. If the scale was in the negative, the day would be amazing because I was closer to being skinnier. I was on the low-carb diet, so I peed on a stick twice a day (sometimes three if I got crazy) to see if I was in optimal ketosis, fat burning mode. I'd chew on **sugar-free gum all day** to curb my appetite. I'd go through packs and packs ~~of gum~~. Mom bought them in bulk from Cosco. She was trying to lose weight, too. I'd strip again, in the evening, and hop on the scale. Then I'd turn on the Style Network and watch models strutting down the runway in expensive clothes and cry.

Nothing ever lasts.

For spring break, I purchased a cheap flight to my grandma's house in the south. I finally arrived and plopped down in a chair at the kitchen table.

"What's wrong?" she placed her palm on the small of my back.

I held back tears. I hadn't eaten that day. "I'm just—I'm so hungry."

She fried shrimp and fries. I ate it. Felt sicker. I wasn't used to the heaviness of food.

After that, I never stopped eating and gained the seventy pounds I'd lost plus some.

Over the last ten years, I've lost some and gained more. On this body awareness rollercoaster, I've hated my body, I've mistreated it, and allowed others to dictate how I felt about it. But I've also loved it, caressed it, celebrated it, and adorned it.

I am at a point where I'm in complete awe of it. The way it breathes for me. Blinks for me. Allows me to type this very essay about it. I'm in love with myself and how it rolls and sways when I move. How it affects others so delightfully.

I'm happier in this fat body than I ever was trying to fit into those jeans that were two or three sizes too small.

My thighs touch. My belly hangs over my panties. My boobs jump when I jump. My double chin greets you before I am able to. My arms squeeze into jackets that don't stretch.

And that is very much so acceptable.

NEW BODY IMAGE
Abigail Thomas

I love being old. I love this new old body of mine. Out of shape, a little overweight, plopped in a chair, I've never been so comfortable, so happy, living in my body. I never weigh myself. I never look in a three-way mirror. I don't care how big my ass looks. I choose my clothes now for comfort and color and texture. I no longer look for the shortest skirts or the tightest sweaters. I don't own a belt, a girdle, a bra, a garter belt or stockings. I no longer ask questions like, "Do these earrings make me look fat?" Those days are over. Nobody looks up when I walk by and that gives me a chance to do my own ogling. It gives me the freedom to see what I notice, and my mind goes off to play where it wants to.

When I was young, my ambition was to be desired. My pursuit was to be pursued. Trivial and shallow, yes, but I was raised in the fifties when snagging a man was the goal. Then the sixties and seventies came along and snagging a whole bunch of men was the goal. I had no problem with my body image. I was young and slender and pretty and I made the most of it. The downside (yes, there was a downside) was self-consciousness I couldn't shake. I couldn't walk down a city street without being aware of who was looking, who was looking back. The problem was that it was all I thought I had, what I concentrated on, what I had to offer. My value. And I believed I had power. The power was partly real, mostly illusory. You can't take a wolf-whistle to the bank, and there was no place for it on my non-existent resume. Don't get me wrong. It didn't suck, but I wasted a lot of time before figuring out who I was, what my strengths might be, something requiring effort, and a different awareness of myself. I wrote this when I was fifty, and it holds even truer today.

"OLD" BODY IMAGE
Abigail Thomas (From *Safekeeping*)

She was sixteen and wearing a tight yellow sweater. It had shrunk, but she had to go to school and nothing else was clean. Her route was along Washington Mews, up University to Fourteenth Street, along Fourteenth to Third Avenue, then up Third to Fifteenth, then one more block east to school. It was a warm fall day. I believe she was also wearing a short plaid skirt, A-line, and probably loafers and no socks. She could never find socks.

The men in New York City, where she had just moved, stared. Some of them put down their tools or else just held them slackly as she walked by. They murmured. My god, she realized. I have power. Like most power it was both utterly real and utterly illusory. But she spent the next forty years with her eye on who was looking back. This didn't get in her way; it was her way. Her ambition was to be desired. Now it's over and what a relief.

Finally, she can get some work done.

HEY, OLD MAN

Dinty W. Moore

I could easily write about finding my body deficient at age twelve, at age twenty, at age thirty-three, and so on, because with each passing year, different aspects of my male physicality have seemed—to me—utterly deficient.

Looking back, I was for the most part wrong, though not always. No one is perfect, after all.

And now, here I am, just a few years short of retirement age, and my body is looking pretty dismal once again. There is the predictable sagging. The bloated middle. The grudging knees. The waning eyesight. Those are to be expected, I suppose. What bothers me most at this juncture are the age spots, hundreds of raised bumps reminding me that the visible surface of what I call "me" has a mind of its own, an outer coating over which I ultimately have very little control.

The spots are properly called seborrheic keratosis; my doctor tells me. He neglects to mention that these little bits of waxy, slightly-elevated skin used to be called "senile warts." They are not warts however, and have no link to senility. Instead, they are just harmless clumps, appearing most prominently among pale-skinned folks of a certain age, especially those who have enjoyed prolonged exposure to the sun. (I'm Irish-American and grew up five minutes from the beach. You can guess how that plays out.)

Unlike other signs of aging, there is no way to exercise these away. The spots appear overnight, stubbornly, like a bitter warning: *Hey, Old Man. Decay is inevitable.*

The body inevitably moves toward decay, a fact that becomes distressingly apparent as we age. And maybe that is at the core of why we so insistently despise our bodies? Unlike our minds, or our spirits, the flesh and muscle we develop over time are clearly on a downward trajectory. Maybe not at first, maybe not at age twelve—but eventually.

Until we die.

I tell myself I'm lucky to have lasted this long. I tell myself, count your blessings, old fellow, it could be so much worse. I tell myself that I'm too old to be vain. Who is even looking? But none of that makes me feel better.

Men don't talk much about this, of course. We preen, exaggerate, deny. But we feel it too.

And yes, it is far worse for women. I grew up in a household surrounded by females, and then married some thirty years ago, and we had one child, a daughter. These women in my life remove any doubt from my mind that it is far more difficult to possess a feminine body, thanks to unachievable expectations, cat-calling, inappropriate stares, shaming, and the constant reminders through advertising of what needs to be concealed or repaired.

Men, they say, grow more distinguished with age. Well sure, if you're tall, thin, wealthy, and graced with natural good looks. For most of us, though, aging means failure, awkwardness, comic belly-fat, bow legs, big sneakers. Age spots.

I work out these days, trying to keep some mobility, some trim. The other day I met a 90-year-old man in the locker room, and he was weighing himself.

"Oh," I said. "I hoped there would a came a day we didn't have to worry about that anymore."

He laughed. "I'm getting my hips replaced." He patted his small gut. "The less strain on the new ones, the better."

So I guess it never ends.

Until it does.

THE RED DOOR: ON BREASTS, PERIODS
AND FEMALE EMPOWERMENT
Pamela Hughes

"…if there is a river more beautiful than this
bright as the blood red edge of the moon…"
~ Lucille Clifton

Poet Lucille Clifton called her uterus her "estrogen kitchen." And of her period, she said, "you / never arrived / splendid in your red dress / without trouble for me." For many women, getting their period does mean trouble. At fifteen, while playing manhunt in the summer darkness with the neighborhood kids, I felt a sudden sharp pain. It hurt so much that I slumped to the curb, hung my head over my waist and gripped my aching stomach with both hands. I hobbled away from game without telling anyone. A few minutes later, while sitting on the toilet, I found that I had received the red badge of discouragement. My period.

I wouldn't tell my mom about getting my period because I was too embarrassed. What she had told us, me, my sister and five brothers, about human reproduction was almost nothing. Instead, she handed us a thin book. At eight years old, I studied it curiously. It held pages of sciency diagrams and basic information. One page showed all the parts of a flower and how it pollinated itself, the pistil and stamen. A few pages later, I saw two chickens on top of each other mating, the internal organs, the male and female cloacae connected. Towards the end, it got to humans. There were separate pages of male and female reproductive organs. On the female diagram, there was no image or mention of the vagina that I remember. And then the diagrams disappeared. The last page showed a man and a woman, covered by a blanket, sleeping side by side on a bed. The caption underneath read, when adults procreate "they sleep close together." I remember those words vividly.

The book created a lot more questions than answers. Like: Could I cross pollinate myself like that flower? And: how exactly did people reproduce? Where were those pictures? Or: Could a girl get pregnant just by sleeping "close together "with someone on a bed? How could that be? No amount of confusion would push me to ask my mom any of these questions. At that point, it would be geography—not botany or biology—that would have the most staying power. For all I knew, my vagina could have been in China.

I don't blame my mom for her lack of guidance. I empathize with her. She probably didn't get any guidance from her own mom, my Sicilian-American grandma, or she from her mother. Silence would teach me—us—to be ashamed of our menstruating bodies, the sexual body. I never got "the talk." Although, I do remember when I was maybe four or five—because I stood at the height of my mom's chest as she sat on the toilet—that she showed me a pad with blood on it. "This is called your menstrual cycle," she explained. She pushed the pad slightly closer to my face and added, "You can have a baby with this." Instead of being horrified, I was mesmerized. I studied the red and wine-colored splotches carefully, looking for any signs of a baby there. I liked baby dolls then and would have loved to have a real baby, so I said, "Well, how can I get some, because I want a baby of my own." She laughed and said that would happen when I was older and married. This would be the last I'd see or hear about menstruation or reproduction directly from her. Apparently, my being a little girl made it easier for my mom to talk about this. Later, my age and her embarrassment shut the door on that topic. This door, the red door, would not open again for me until high school, when man hunt would turn into woman found.

I was a sophomore in high school when I got "it." My uterus had started to cook up my hormones late. That's when my body started growing strange stuff on it. When hairs started sprouting on my armpits and between and on that part of the body that my sister and I, as girls and adolescents, called our pee pee, this seemed very, very weird. I remember thinking, *yuck! It's ugly to be furry in places where I was smooth before.* This metamorphosis held the same kind of awfulness that turning into a giant beetle would, until I got used to the shape of my new skin, soft protuberances and bleeding without an entry wound.

Before the actual physical pain of getting my period, other things start to hurt. My breasts ached when they started coming in, like two small pits stuck under my skin, blooming directly from seed to fruit, sans stem, leaves or tree. Some possibilities are plums, peaches, grapefruits, cantaloupes, and watermelons. We are farmers, us women. Children are the next crop. As a mom now, I can tell you that we want our "harvest" alive and well, happy and thriving. We don't want our children killed in wars or by violence, prejudice and bullets.

I stopped aching and growing at peaches, size B to C, depending on my weight. I still found myself asking, *Where will all this growing take me?* I didn't know, could only glean information from the girls around me. My sister, who was a year younger, got her period first, around two years earlier. As it turned out she, didn't know much either. What I *did* know was that in having five brothers, I was more a boy then a girl. I liked climbing trees, and the occasional fist fight, so even though I wanted to get my period—to be like other girls—it was a bittersweet moment which meant restricting myself, not running as fast or running at all (before I started using tampons) or being able to swim. If a tampon or a pad commercial appeared on the screen as my family watched TV together, I would cringe in horror and humiliation. And hope that I could disappear into thin air. Without a constructive coming of age ritual or a supportive narrative from my mom, it was embarrassing to bleed in America.

A woman bleeding was trouble in many male-dominated countries around the world. It perceived seen as dirty, dangerous, something to be hidden. Within three of the world's major religions, Christianity, Judaism and Islam, a menstruating woman was considered ritually unclean, so women were not allowed to participate in ceremonies or touch the holy books, the Bible, Torah or Koran. As a non-participant, she was powerless. It is the same in many cultures across the world; women's menses are often seen as impure, as a kind of pollution, so

194

myriad cleanliness rules and restrictions have been and are still imposed. To site just a few examples, in the Roma society, i.e., "gypsy" [sic], a menstruating woman has to be separated from the men, use different soap for washing herself, never handle a man's clothing or allow her skirt to touch a man or male child. She cannot cook or touch the dishes used by her family. If a male is touched by her, he could become *marime,* unclean himself and be out-casted from his *kumpania* or tribe. Similarly, in Niger, a woman who is menstruating must not handle cooking utensils or anything related to eating or food. There are also cultures, like the Native Americans, that revere menarche (the first period) and see it as powerful rite of passage. The Apaches hold a four-day sunrise ceremony, a coming of age ritual, to celebrate a girl's transition to womanhood. Many Native American tribes, like the Apache, had matriarchal roots, where women could be honored leaders, so we could see where this reverence sprung. In certain Hindu sects, a girl's first period is also celebrated during another coming of age ritual called the *Ritu Kala Samskara,* while in Ghana, the girls of the Bono people are given special ceremonial dresses, sacred beads and are sung to by their elders during a weeklong ceremony and feast. However, in many places of the non-Western and Westernized world, the menses on the whole are still a clotted, closeted affair. Luckily, this is beginning to change.

With the advent of Eve Ensler's monologues, the vagina has become a dialogue. Where guys might talk about their penises openly to other guys, though perhaps in joking or sanctified tones going back through the centuries from the Shakespearian "staff," or in worship of the monumental show of the Greek fertility god Priapus' phallic manhood, or the seven-foot pink penis riding high in a modern day Japanese fertility parade, women did not discuss their parts until more recently. Now I hear Millennials talking about their vaginas with candor: the vag, (pronounced like Madge) vagagay, her V, or simply, my vagina. While in the parking lot on campus, I overheard one of my college freshmen nonchalantly talking about her vagina to another female student. "My vagina is happy today," she said. Being on my way into class, I didn't hear why it was happy, but I was just glad it was.

Then there was Snooki from the reality show, *Jersey Shore,* when she exclaimed, while drunkenly riding a bike on the Seaside Heights boardwalk, "Oh my god, my vagina is falling out!" I had to laugh, to honor such silliness and profundity. Where would it fall to? And would she be able to get it back? I hoped so.

The new dialogue has brought women's parts out into the air, both literally and figuratively, via pop culture, art and literature: as vagina lollipops, jewelry, sculptures, paintings and in plays and poetry. Japanese artist, Megumi Igarashi, went as far as to display her vagina in public. Like many women, she had never seen her own vagina, so she created a mold of hers and started to apply it as 3-D art, to household articles like phone cases, and finally a kayak. While in Japan, during the *Kanamara Matsuri* (the Festival of the Steel Phallus) it is seen as life affirming to parade portable penis shrines up to seven feet tall through the streets, Megumi was arrested and convicted of obscenity charges. Twice. She had stepped her vagina out of line and had to pay the price, a 3595 dollar fine. But such penalties won't stop progress. The vagini is out of the bottle. The new discourse puts our reproductive organs in a place of daily discussion and honor.

How the story is told shapes the narrative—the new story of our bodies, shows ownership and speaks of a place of power. It is a harbinger that we are moving from patriarchy to a more women-centered society, an equilibrium of female and male power. Like uncontrolled estrogen or testosterone in the physical body, which leads to imbalance, illness, and even death, the same goes for the world body. We are out of kilter. As Leon F. Seltzer, Ph.D, wrote in his article, "The Testosterone Curse," found in *Psychology Today*:

> At its worst, high-T [testosterone] dominance and competitiveness can involve brute force, violence, and fighting behavior of all kinds...High-T males can be "rough and callous." Their more tender feelings literally "blunted" by elevated testosterone levels, they tend not to be particularly concerned about—or, for that matter, *interested* in—the feelings of others. And unmoderated feelings such as lust,

resentment, or <u>rage</u> can easily preempt the softer feelings of <u>love</u>, compassion, or <u>forgiveness</u>. It's similar to men on steroids, especially vulnerable to being "taken over" by powerful feelings—the reason that the term "roid rage"

Hi-T dominance, as we see in the world today in regard to perpetual war, kills. We need more estrogen at the helm to restore the balance. After all, the estrogen kitchen is a wonderful place where radical physical transformation occurs. The estrogen office and the estrogen ballot booth are wonderful places where radical transformation will also occur. The Dali Lama said that women would save the world.

I knew this long before he said it.

To be more specific, the Dali Lama said, "The world will be saved by the Western woman." Though he didn't explain this statement further, this is the way I see it. Going back to the ancient Greeks, Western male-dominated society has created a legacy of war, the colonization and exploitation of countries and peoples, slavery, the oppression of women and "people of color," environmental degradation (stemming from the biblical ethic that man shall have dominion over the earth and all its creatures), as well as nuclear weapons that could kill us all, so it only makes sense that Western women, who have educated and empowered themselves, will play a role in counterbalancing this. Though Western women may spearhead the process, it will be *all* women of every kind, country, color and shape that will help change the world for the better. There will be no violent revolution or take over, the oppression of men—guys barefoot and pregnant in the kitchen. The problems that we face may be as monolithic as the Washington Monument, but can overcome them. Along with continued public (and pubic) discourse, change will come on the platforms of: social justice; transforming colonial and neocolonial systems and biases; education and literacy; true democracy; non-violence; intersectionality; gender and racial equality; LGBTQ civil rights; myriad diverse women being in leadership and governmental roles worldwide; intellectual and internet freedoms; renewable energy;

environmentally and health-friendly sustainable food sources; eco-awareness and the careful stewardship of our earth. Combined with activism and grassroots movements, these changes will happen gradually and naturally, a sort of creeping velvet evolution.

As the new story continues, as the dislike of our bodies is replaced by reverence, as each new generation of breasts continues to grow and blood—*life affirming blood*—continues to flow, more and more women will step on the threshold of the red door with aplomb, to fling it open and stand empowered and *empowering* anywhere in the world.

ON VARICOSE VEINS

s. Nicholas

At a July barbecue twelve years ago, I wore short-shorts. Even though I hadn't had a chance to really tan yet, and I was exhausted and didn't want to shave my legs, and I was a Single-Mom-With-Two-Kids. I wore them because, at 5'3, my legs somehow seemed longer, leaner, in short-shorts. As if I could be a dancer. As if I could walk the runway. And he was there. I'm pretty sure it was those shorts on my ass that gave me the confidence to touch his knee lightly and laugh at a funny joke, to tuck my hair behind my ear like in the movies, to smile the way everyone who doesn't know me always tells me to smile. Because I imagined I could be a dancer. Even though I was a Single-Mom- With-Two-Kids. He walked me to my car. And the rest is over a decade of history.

Now Married-With-Three-Kids, I can't wear short-shorts. Or capris, or even slightly longer skirts. What began as thick green rivers down the backs of my knees have grown to include streams and small purple eddies spiraling around my thighs and looping carelessly down to my ankles. As if they were drunken, red, ink doodles. Or thin galaxies. My husband doesn't run his fingers over those veins the way he does my scars and stretch marks. They lead nowhere. There is no fight behind them. No story of strength and perseverance. They slowly map hours on the elliptical, shuffled half-asleep steps, taken at midnight while rocking a crying, colicky infant, trips across the parking lot with bags of groceries, or my pacing anger around our bedroom. They are only weak, those vessels.

My best memories are not footsteps. It's not my body upright.

I know, it is partly the fault of my heart. Always pushing and pulling my blood, out and then back in, so quickly, so forcefully. Always beating so fiercely. Those fragile veins, surfacing calmly, nearly unnoticed, these last few years, more quietly than a mole, easier than squandered summer, are a contrast to my defiant heart. It screams at me to continue living. To fear, to love, to rejoice. And my veins reply that I am tired, and old.

I want to love them. But unlike most everything else in my life, the desire to love them does not make it so. I tell myself that the weeds in my garden are eager and stubborn, and I love them for it. I wrap my arms around family members that I cannot reconcile with, and will myself to love them. June bugs skittering up the window screens, are drawn to light, and for that, they earn my love. But these ugly, useless varicose veins, I cover them. I wear jeans on the hottest of summer days, and leggings to the gym. I place my naked limbs quickly under the sheets at night and stare furiously at them while sitting on the toilet. I fantasize about expensive surgeries, compression stockings, and time travel.

Some things, perhaps, require familiarity, before they can be loved. So I've made a promise to myself, to become acquainted with my middle-aged, no short-shorts legs, and these veins that have given up under the weight of my life. To trace their squiggles and twists, until they are mine. Not my mother's, not my grandmother's, but my bursting, curving streaks. Maybe then, I can love them. These threads of a life spent moving, and sometimes even, dancing.

MERMAIDS DON'T READ JANE AUSTEN NOVELS

Heather Lang

Pearl wiggles around in the bathtub, just a bit. Her mermaid tail sways naturally with each turn of the paperback's page. Her fins unfold with every lift of sweet peppermint tea.

It's not unusual to find a stack of books near the bathtub. Some are meant for reading, and others are only there as a pedestal, something to raise up the teacup just a few more inches. Then, it's easier to reach the ceramic vessel, which is both singular and perfect. Even the hairline fracture lends itself to the teacup's paisley delight.

Pearl's body relaxes in the water. Her periwinkle eyes are clamshell wide. Pearl's arms stretch elegantly, and her skin's porcelain-pale. She's beautiful, but more than that, really, she's mermaid-gorgeous.

This fiberglass bathtub is nothing like the claw foot tub in which she previously bathed. The blushing pink gave off a hue so sweet that bouquets of vanilla seemed to waft from the porcelain, even when a bubble bath had not been drawn. Her new tub, on the other hand, is rather rectangular, and its prescription-pill white. The jutting-out showerhead is too angular to be pretty. The bathing area's sealed shut by its curtains of sticky plastic, and the grout between wall tiles has been stained by hair dye.

Pearl, however, does not care about the bathtub, nor is she interested in who marries who in Pride and Prejudice. She also fails to take interest in the high water bill—although, arguably, she should, for she lives in the desert. But Pearl is not a thinker, or a doer or a dreamer.

I suppose it isn't fair of me to write this about poor Pearl, even though she is, quite literally, unable to care. This mermaid's a tattoo, existing on the innermost section of my right arm. When I turn the page of a novel, Pearl breaches the water and then sinks back just below the surface.

Pearl wears hot pink lipstick and ocean-blue eye shadow. On my own face, you'll find none. When I'm wearing makeup, I don't feel like myself. When I'm feeling self- conscious, I sometimes make jokes: "My mermaid wears mascara for the both of us—this way, I don't have to!" Sometimes I wink. I hide behind my petite Pearl from time to time. This is something that I know about myself, and it's something with which I'm quite all right.

Pearl first "moved in" roughly seven years ago. Since then, my body has changed.

I've entered my thirties. I've moved to Nevada, and grown chubby and content. I am at home here, a more truthful version of the fat-and-happy adage. As a tradeoff, I feel anxious less frequently. Much less so than I did in my twenties, but I still tend to stress eat when the going does get tough.

Pearl's changed, too. Our curves are, well, curvier. Yet, she never struggles with feeling like a sea manatee. This being said, I can't call Pearl lucky. She can't enjoy the bathwater or the sweet peppermint tea, and she can't daydream about Georgiana's pianoforte from the Jane Austen novel.

As I get older, I consider my own body a vessel, something that carries me from place to place, from book to book, from hug to hug. Like my favorite teacup with its hairline fracture, I am uniquely flawed, delicate, but full with purpose. In a way, it is everything. Yet, I don't love the look of my figure, especially during these chubbier years. But when I want to eat poorly, to skip a long walk, or to work beyond exhaustion, it helps me to remember that my body is a vessel through which I experience the world, and because of it I can do all of the things that I daydream Pearl might like to do. Moreover, it helps me remember that I am not alone. A mermaid lives here, too.

THE DAILY BATH

Zorida Mohammed

In her last days, when she could no longer move around on her own, one of the few things my mother looked forward to was her daily bath. She had taken to speaking only when absolutely necessary. If she thought we were tardy getting to her bath, she'd shake her towel at us when we went past her room. It took two of my sibs round the clock to care for her. Her 11 times baby-birthing body was fraying, and tore in places when she was touched.

After I tried to help her off the toilet one day, holding her around the waist, her skin gave. When blood sprang up in the spaces where her skin had been, I let go of her, and she slid to the floor. It took three of us to figure out how to get her into her wheelchair without further breaching her skin. Eventually, she had to be bathed in her bed.

I was familiar with my mother's body, the folds of skin on her sides, her always small and shapely waist, the white, wavy striations on her legs and on her stretched-out belly. She had many tiny black skin taggy things around her neck. Her face remained without a line or wrinkle. She was quite possibly the prettiest woman in the village, and she loved beautiful clothes, which she had paid for on terms. Her long black hair was now salt and pepper, and fluffed around her face when loose.

My mother's breasts are a bejesus of a story unto themselves. It was hard to image that they were once lovely orbs. Later, they hung like plump eggplants, and now they just laid flat: thick speckled skin sacks reaching past her waist.

The first time it was my turn to bathe her, my mother protested mildly, preferring my sister who'd been her bather-in-chief. I stepped up as if I knew what to do. My sister soaped and rinsed the washrag and guided me. I washed her body in sections, beginning with her face. When I got to her private parts, I felt as if I were intruding. I parted her labia and all my nervousness disappeared into a momentary but intense focus when I discovered her dusky purplish flower hidden dormant between her legs. Her body had somehow reconstituted itself to her pre-baby days. There were no stretch marks, no evidence that I or anyone else had pushed their way through that purple passage.

TEDDY-BEAR THEATER
Kaylie Jones

I was already in a bad mood from having to stop writing in the middle of a paragraph. I'd forgotten to set my alarm, which normally gave me ample time every week-day afternoon to pull myself together and clear my head of the made-up world of my book, and get to my daughter's preschool before the dismissal bell rang.

I was now late, and it was the middle of February and freezing, and there were no cabs, and I had to run all the way to Park Avenue, and I was drenched inside my down coat by the time I reached the outer double doors of the International Preschools. Only one of the doors was open, as usual, which seemed absurd to me. Most of the mommies and nannies were already outside, with a few still coming out. I had to time my entry through the one open door, feeling a bit like an old, beat-up car pulling onto a fast highway.

In the vestibule, the last of the little ones were already strapped into their strollers in their heavy winter coats and hats. The Palestinian nanny in her abaya and hijab was refusing to move out of the way of the Israeli nanny, who was trying to squeeze through the door with her stroller, but she would not ask the Palestinian nanny to move because they did not speak.

My daughter was still with Miss Beth, holding her hand at the top of the landing, the last child waiting. My heart began to slide up into my throat, a weird, primal reaction to seeing my daughter's anxious face. I had never been late before. My mother used to forget to pick me up at school when I was little and by the time I could reach my nanny Judite on the phone, night had fallen and only the janitor and the principal were left, the school echoing emptily, deserted. This memory caused me such anxiety that I always set my alarm, which today for some inexplicable reason, I had forgotten to do.

I rushed up the steps and hugged my daughter, apparently too tightly, because she squirmed in my arms. I let go and smiled up apologetically at Miss Beth, then led my girl down the steps by the hand, to her stroller that was folded up and parked under her cubby hole. I opened the stroller one-handed and sat her down but she fought me so I held her down and buckled the safety strap. I just wanted to get out of there. I was still sweating mightily inside my own down coat, and the heat that prickled outward from my chest and crept up my neck felt too much like anger.

I tried to force my daughter's arm through the sleeve of her pink coat with yellow butterflies but she kicked at me shouting, "No!" There was real fury in her tone and I had no idea why. Why are you doing this to me? Why are you rejecting me? I'm not like my mother, I didn't forget you. I'm here, aren't I?

"No!" she shouted again, kicking my forearms with her stout little boots. Something within me snapped, and my arm shot out of its own volition.

Whack.

The slap was so loud all the faces turned toward me—the last of the moms and nannies and even the little ones, strapped safely into their seats. Miss Beth was gone, back upstairs, having handed off the last of her charges. Thank God. But, holy shit, I'd slapped my girl much too hard. There was a moment of total silence, and then my daughter began to howl.

I swiftly pushed her stroller toward the door as she screamed and kicked and thrashed her arms. I was still gripping her coat in one fist along with the stroller's handlebar. I pushed the Palestinian nanny and the Israeli nanny out of the way because damn them and their stupid war, and charged down Park Avenue in the wrong direction.

My daughter's howling did not cease. Finally, I stopped her stroller at a corner, a safe distance from the school, and crouched before her. Her face was twisted into an expression of such shock and despair that her features were unrecognizable. Or perhaps it was that she did not recognize me. She had red finger marks on her cheek from where my hand had landed.

"I'm so sorry, baby girl. I don't know what happened to me. I don't know why I did that."

"I'm telling Daddy!" she wailed.

I considered telling her not to tell her daddy. But then I realized that this was how it had started with my mother. I was never to tell my daddy. This was our understanding. But I did tell my father, as best I could, bringing up when we were alone together, which was not often, examples of injustices committed against me by my mother. I suppose he must have discussed them with her, because the next time she assaulted me with her poisoned arrows, her words were ten times more violent, more poisonous, and not a single one would miss its mark. She could be kind and tender too, which made me drop my guard. She could always tell when I dropped my guard, and that was when she would strike.

Still breathing heavily, still sweating inside my coat, I said, "Please, honey, put your coat on. It's cold." I held it out to her. Finally, she lifted her arms and allowed me to slip them through the sleeves. I zipped up the coat, put her hat on her head and her hands in her mittens, and we began our long walk home.

During our six-block trek east, I ruminated. I was seven years sober now, and I thought I'd done all the work. I went to meetings five days a week. I'd made my amends. I'd learned self-control. But something was clearly wrong with me. *No*, said the comforting voice of denial, *you are perfectly normal. That was a normal reaction.* By the time we reached our Yorkville neighborhood, I had practically convinced myself. Maybe I would not need to tell my husband after all.

When we got inside, I asked my girl if she wanted to do puzzles together. No. Well, did she want to play with her American Girl Dolls with me? No. Did she want to sit with me on the couch and watch this morning's *Sesame Street* again? No. How about an ice-cream? Yes! We never had ice-cream until after her dinner, but what harm could one ice cream do? I peeled down the wrapper on an ice cream sandwich, leaving some paper at the bottom, and handed it to her; she wandered off into her room. Her room was very small and narrow, but a good friend of mine who was a carpenter and a sailor had built her a seaman's loft bed with a railing, with steps that were not ladder-like, and a desk and huge toy cabinet with shelves underneath. She had her own TV on a dresser, which she could watch from the bed or the floor.

I heard the TV go on. It was not hooked up to cable, but she had a stack of CDs she knew how to insert by herself. Familiar music wafted through the apartment; it was her favorite movie, about a little girl in a red dress who dreams she enters a world filled with strange but friendly characters, a talking red bear and a human-sized talking dog, who befriend her and teach her how to sing and dance, and together they put on a show.

I sat on the couch staring into space for a long time as darkness fell, and I didn't know what to do with myself. Finally, I flicked on a lamp, and its soft amber glow created a circle of light around me. The books stacked three deep on the wall-to-wall bookcase became visible. My bedroom as a child in Paris had wall-to-wall bookcases, filled with the leftover paperbacks of my dad's that hadn't fit in the wall-to-wall bookcases in the living room. The smell of old books had always comforted me.

After a while I rose to prepare my girl's dinner, organic chicken nuggets, green peas, rice and corn. Nightfall was the hardest time, that in-between time when day is done and a drink is in order, to soothe and ease the tensions, the stress. But... what stress? What possible stress could have caused me to overreact in this way? I had never hit her before. But if there's a first time there will always be another; I'd learned this in recovery. My rage had come upon me just like an alcoholic blackout, with no thought, no control on my part.

But this was an isolated incident, said that comforting voice in my head. It'll never happen again ...

While her chicken nuggets toasted, I went to the fridge and popped a can of Diet Coke, sliced up a lime and squeezed it over ice cubes in a delicate, hand-blown blue glass, the last survivor of the six my husband and I had bought in Mexico on a scuba diving expedition, long before our girl was born.

I put her dinner on her alphabet tray with a sippy cup of milk, a napkin and a spoon. She'd never once had baby formula; I'd nursed her for two years. Wasn't that dedication? Wasn't that a sign of self-sacrifice? Of good mothering skills? My mother liked to tell the story of how she'd nursed me for three months, until the night JFK was elected. They were out at Harry's Bar in Paris with the other leftie expat Americans, waiting for the election results. She got drunk, but now I assume that meant drunker than usual, and she called home to tell my nanny Judite to give me a bottle.

During the two years I nursed my girl, my mother liked to say, "Are you going to get a dorm room next to hers when she goes to college so you can keep nursing her?" I had never yet been able to unfreeze myself enough to come up with an appropriate response. If I'd been able to laugh at her barbs the way my brother did, it would have been so much better.

I entered my girl's room carrying her tray and for a moment I stood paralyzed in the doorway. She had taken all her chairs—her two small table chairs, her child's desk chair, an American Girl doll couch, and her beanbag chair—and lined them up in two rows in front of the TV. In them sat her three American Girl dolls, and her large stuffed animals, a bear, and a soft, mushy zebra my mother had given her, a white rabbit, and a hippopotamus ballerina in a pink tutu. Below them, on the floor, she'd arrayed the smaller animals and dolls, and they all sat, a rapt audience, watching the TV screen with their glassy eyes. My throat constricted and I felt tears threatening.

"What is this?" I asked in an unnaturally high voice.

"It's Teddy Bear Theater," she replied. "We're watching together so I'm not alone."

We'd never stopped trying to have another child; having her at 37, I had already been almost too old, and her birth was a messy and difficult affair, ending after 24 hours of labor in an emergency c-section. But she was not talking about being an only child. She was talking about being lonely.

I set her tray down on the little table and got down on the floor and crossed my legs in front of the TV. I lifted her onto my lap and she didn't resist. The smell of baby shampoo wafted up comfortingly through my nostrils.

"Can I tell you something?" I asked, my voice quivering. "It's important."

After a long silence, she said, "What?"

"I'm sorry you feel lonely. Sometimes I feel lonely too. I'm sorry I got angry at you earlier and I'm sorry I slapped you. I was late because I was writing and I forgot to set my alarm."

"Why do you love your writing more than me?"

"I don't. I love you more than anything in the world. My writing is different. It's my work. Sometimes I get so focused I lose myself." By now I'd stopped trying to contain my tears and she turned her face away from the TV to gaze at me with an expression both curious and concerned.

"I don't think you should write anymore," she said, quite equably.

At that moment, we heard the key turn in the front door. Her father was home. As soon as he'd set down his work bag and his keys, he came in to find us. He stood in the doorway of her room much as I had, surprised by the scene before him; he looked so grown-up and capable in his consignment shop charcoal-gray cashmere overcoat and sports jacket.

"What's going on?" he asked.

"I was late to pick her up and we were both upset. And... I slapped her... much too hard." I watched his face, expecting judgment, but all I saw there was concern, and his bottomless love that never judged me, unless he was at the high peak of one of his bi-polar cycles. Then he was a different person entirely.

"I need help," I said.

After I gave our girl her bath, I stretched out on her bed with her and read her extra story books and held her until long after she was asleep. This, when I was little, had been my nanny Judite's purview. I'd beg her to stay, stay, please stay with me. Sometimes, not often, she'd fall asleep before I did, stretched out beside me after her long day of drudgery, and these occasions seemed to me a marvelous reprieve, like Christmas.

The next evening, my husband came home quite late after his group therapy and said, "I got you a book." I could see from the tentative way he was standing in the living room doorway that he was expecting resistance. I did not resist and nodded in silence.

He went back out to the kitchen, where he'd left his work bag. A moment later he was back, a shiny white paperback dangling loosely in his hand. I reached out to take it.

Giving the Love that Heals: A Guide for Parents, by Harville Hendrix, PhD.

"A guy in my group recommended it," he said, adding quickly, "he has two kids."

Later, in the deepest hours of the night, after too many reruns of *Law & Order*, when the city was finally quiet, I got into bed, my husband long asleep, and cracked open the book. In the introduction, Dr. Hendrix congratulated the reader, for she had opened the book, which was the first and most difficult step, and meant that she was ready to begin the long and painful journey toward changing the toxic patterns of her own childhood.

AN EMAIL IN MY DRAFTS FOLDER
Amber Moore

Dear Harold III,

This is not your name. I've assigned you a new one to continue to protect you. You're welcome.

I'm writing to you this email I'll never send because I've been thinking about you lately. I'm teaching my students a book about a teenage rape survivor. They need to read stories like ours.

That night, the sun seemed to come down mid-sentence. Have you remodeled the memory of that evening in your mind? Do you tell yourself that I wanted you, that I was caught in a current of champagne? Let me assure you; you're wrong. I was passed out naked, waiting for him, not you. When you crawled in and kissed my neck, I assumed whose lips those were. I did think it was strange that he would grab at me like that, and when your stubby dry fingers stabbed inside me, I gasped and there you were.

I don't really remember what happened in the next few minutes but I'm certain of how I felt. The alcohol still pounding through my bloodstream seemed to form a protective layer, keeping me from full awareness. I started crying fat tears filled with Maybelline Lasting Drama Blackest Black that dripped off my nose, snuck around the side of my face to disappear into my neck, my hair, like you did. You slapped and squeezed, your spittle cooling my flushed back, watering my bowed bluebells tattoo on my right shoulder blade. They shook as I trembled.

To evade your hands, I rolled to the edge of the bed, beside the cold wall with the drafty window of unsympathetic icy panes. The frosted glass was complicit in keeping this secret too.

You were muttering, clawing, when another boy opened the door. Light flooded into the room accusingly. He was our friend, but right then, he was more mine. He paused in the doorframe and in a tone I've never heard him use before or since, he told you to get *out*.

You both left. I told myself it could have been worse but still, I shook. Minutes later, my now-husband threw open the door looking wild. Crossing the room in two strides, he collected me in his arms and held tightly, asking what was wrong, he said downstairs that something happened, what is it, take a breath, tell me…

I cried for hours, leaving my eyelids swollen and hot. Suddenly, my body seemed on fire and I felt swollen, as if I was allergic to you. I apologized while he shushed me and I begged him not to find you and beat you, to stay with me, please.

If I ever do send this to you, I don't want an apology. Regrets grow tiresome. Don't be relieved that I never said anything. Your job now is to do better if you can manage. It might save you from yourself, and save other women from a story like ours, or worse.

MY HUSBAND'S HABIT
Susan Shapiro

"Try my shrimp tempura." He offered a chopstick-full.

"I don't need another Jewish mother," I told my tall 40-year-old blind date, who'd ordered the most fattening dish on the Japanese menu.

"You're not a veggie-lover who does disco aerobics and runs miles on treadmills going nowhere?" he asked, sarcastically.

I ate my steamed broccoli, rolling my eyes, thinking: he sounds just like my brothers.

The winter of 1990, I was a broke 29-year-old journalist, five foot seven, 128 pounds, size six. Hardly a health nut, I smoked, drank, partied. From a Midwest clan of serious eaters, I'd always wrestled with my weight. In Manhattan, I'd finally found a strict food and workout regimen, proud to be the most in-shape Shapiro.

He was a TV/film comedy guy from Westchester who had 11 years and 150 pounds on me. I nicknamed him Batman, who was his favorite superhero "because he doesn't have superpowers, he gives himself power," he explained. I was drawn to his handsome face, chestnut eyes, long curly hair I could run my fingers through. I liked his six foot four frame, sardonic humor, John O'Hara references, and questions about my book column. I did not like his oversized jeans, untied sneakers, untucked flannel shirt hiding a big tummy. Or his complaint, escorting me home: "You walk too fast."

"You walk too slow."

At my door, he surprised me with a warm bear hug and long, deep lip-lock that made my toes tingle. Still I didn't want a partner who'd fit perfectly into the family I'd escaped.

"Sweet, smart but not really my type," I reported to the married friend who'd fixed us up.

214

"Your type is neurotic, self-destructive and not interested in you," she said. "This one is brilliant AND a mensch. Try him again."

"But he's a hog! His favorite food groups are pizza, burgers, fries and beer, like my brothers. He makes fun of exercise."

"Your last guy was a slim, athletic cheater who dumped you," she recalled.

I was still hung up on "Hamlet," a theatre director who was my age, six feet, 160 pounds. We ate light, exercised daily. For the year and a half we dated, I was leaner, more toned. He romanced me in Jamaica, where we hiked, swam laps, snorkeled. Back in New York, when we strode briskly down the street, someone commented: "What a beautiful couple." Dumb reason to pledge your life to someone. Yet it seemed magical, like I'd left the Borscht Belt for a wispy, WASPy Vermont Ralph Lauren ad.

Going from chubby nerd in grade school to being in a fit duet felt glorious. I stopped joking about not wanting to sleep with a guy who had better thighs than I did. Until Hamlet left me for a wispier actress. Taken with Hamlet's external sheen, I'd ignored our internal dysfunction. I was devastated (remembering Ralph Lauren was really Ralph Lifshitz from the Bronx.)

Batman's arms caught me. For months, we laughed and argued at plays, movies, meals he treated for. I gave him copies of hard covers I'd reviewed. We fooled around but didn't go to bed. I was attracted yet ambivalent, pining for my former flame. When Batman mentioned his ex-girlfriend called him around the same time Hamlet phoned to say he missed me, I took it as a sign. I bolted back to my old boyfriend. We were slim, sexy, in sync. Until Hamlet fell for a different actress. Again!

Heartbroken, I hid behind work—for three years. Interviewing an oversized TV star on his Broadway debut, I met his petite wife and brood, a few kids from her first union the star had adopted. "I'm so lucky I found the smartest, sweetest, most generous guy," she beamed. I had too, but I'd ruined it. In my early thirties, I realized what was fun for a short-term honey was different from a husband. Batman didn't need to change size. I needed to change perspective.

I recalled Batman. He was still single too, and wanted to see me. For our reunion, I jumped him on his torn mattress on the floor of his cramped one-bedroom. He was hot, open, hilarious. I'd never associated carnal bliss with comfort before. How self- conscious I'd been with Hamlet, holding in my stomach, reaching for a nightgown to cover up. With Batman, I felt freer, looser, 11 years better looking.

Yet for the next two years, I struggled with our age and diet differences. I don't know when I decided he was mine—all 280 pounds of him. Maybe when he schlepped sour dills from the Lower East Side on the plane to meet my parents, smelling like pickle juice. Or the week, despite tight deadlines, he took my visiting brother, another foodie I'd labeled "waiter's dream," to dinner six nights in a row, so my sibling wouldn't feel lonely in a strange town.

Right before our late Saturday night Soho wedding reception, I took three aerobics classes in a row. "What are you doing later?" the instructor asked. "Getting married." He laughed. "I'm not kidding."

On our Jamaica honeymoon, hoping to reinvent picturesque memories, I swam laps in a white bikini, snorkeled, hiked, gathered exotic shells on my own. Batman sat by the pool, reading thrillers, scoping out eateries advertising specials on salt-fish fritters, sweet potato casserole, chicken fricassee. Oy! His idea of romance was all-you-can-eat restaurants.

Rather than exercise or cease carb loading, he trashed my habits, insisting I stop smoking, drinking, partying. Not because I'd live longer, because "I can't stand those drunk idiots you hang out with and hate the smell of smoke." Since he was demanding I stop being self-destructive, I retaliated. "Then you have to quit junk food!" He only quit bringing it home.

After I kicked cigarettes, my long-term appetite-suppressant, I ate even more vigilantly. At an Indian café, he ordered garlic naan, toasted poori AND paratha stuffed with potatoes. We argued. I walked out. Two therapy sessions later, it was decreed: he'd go bread-crazy with others; with wife, he'd suppress starch. On my birthday, we nibbled broiled seafood. He gave up grease and batter for that night annually.

Returning from Peter Luger with a pal, he boasted they'd finished half a steer. I teased "make the pig noise." He oinked accordingly. But the more I fixed myself, the less I noticed his weight. The longer we lasted, the better we lusted.

Then everything changed the year I turned fifty. My father got sick. My editor dumped me. My long-term therapist relocated. Kickboxing to overcompensate, I tore two ligaments in my lower back. I couldn't work out—for two years. I gained 15 pounds. Size 10 or 12 was normal, but I didn't feel lithe and lovely anymore. I focused on reconnecting with family, helping students, charity, my husband.

Taking me to see *Iron Man* for his birthday, Batman slipped and fell on buttered popcorn at the theatre. "Guess this proves I'm not a superhero," he said, incurring his own spinal injury, conceding food was doing him in. Worried he couldn't fly or walk well on an upcoming Asian business trip, my cute couch potato of 18 years shocked me by reducing. Quickly.

One day he greeted me in his old jeans. "40 waist are too big," he showed off the extra room. Two weeks later: "Hey, these 38s fit. My 36s look good, don't they?" He modeled shirts and blazers from college that now buttoned. He lost twenty pounds before his trip. Within six months he was down fifty more, seriously slim, which he demanded I tell him. Thrice daily.

"Do I still look thin?" he asked, eating Greek yogurt that replaced his bagel.

"You look amazing," I said, honestly.

His wedding ring slid off his smaller finger. Uh oh. I recalled my exes' penchant for eye candy, worried Batman would prefer tiny actresses in his industry, afraid I'd lost my allure.

"Susan, if I ever cheated on you, it would be with pizza."

I smiled. Yet I was resentful, used to being svelter. I longed for my frayed Levis to fit.

Premenopausal, I nixed fruit juice, frozen yogurt and weight trained daily while Batman's diet consisted of: quitting fried crap. He'd

217

become hot while I was hot flashing; I feared I was aging horribly, Jack Sprat and his butterball wife. If my dinner was four sushi rolls with rice like his, I'd pork out. It wasn't fair. In pictures he was trim and chic; I was jowly. Frustrated, I binged on *Orange is the New Black* and popcorn, making him a bowl. When I was the diet shrew that would have thrilled him. Now I was the bad influence. He had the nerve to eat a few kernels, then stop. I finished his too. He mocked me with "oink."

Yet Batman liked the extra meat on me. "You look beautiful, the same as the day we met."

"I do not!" I screamed. "I look hideous."

"You're right, you're hideous," he said, and we kissed. His contentment with me made me more comfortable. Still, I consulted a Jungian astrologer who confirmed the switch was astral: Batman was under a Uranus moon which kept him skinny, whereas I had a lot of lucky Jupiter—a big planet that apparently made you successful but chubby.

Last month, getting an MRI to check my spine injury, I feared I'd get claustrophobic in the coffin-like machine. Batman insisted on coming. As my lower half was scanned in the tunnel, my better half sat beside me, adjusted my headphones piping Bob Dylan, caressing my hair for an hour, calming me. It was the most romantic gesture ever, the size of our love all that mattered.

Afterwards, eating Indian food, we shared one piece of garlic naan. Then we shuffled home at his snail pace, arm in arm.

CELL MEMORY

Jennifer Kircher Carr

The body remembers: every mile run, sunscreen applied or not, children borne or not, piercings of the ears or brow or nose, tattoos of small flowers on the ankle, first star seen and related wish. Every love. Every attempted love. Every first love that was real and you could hold it and it wracked through your body then you could sigh and smile and think this is the meaning of life. Every person you thought you would die if you didn't hear from them again. Every voice lost to history, every smile to memory. Every finger brushing your cheek, every hand holding your own.

My dear body, how I have loved you.

All the years we have run the pavement together. All the long walks through sunlit fields, following the dog. All the mornings misty over the hill, the birds calling to each other from the trees. Sitting on cold grass by the lake, watching the gulls.

All the time spent in the garden, rearranging plants the way some rearrange furniture, the earthy smell as we tilled the soil, the satisfying slice as we split the hostas, the careful mining of baby bleeding hearts, the digging for them of new homes. All the pulling of pachysandra creeping too close to the stones of family graves.

My body, you have borne me two beautiful daughters, and harbored me many loves. We have smelled lilacs in the air and tugged velvety blankets over us as we settled on the couch for favorite movies.

I have fond memories of you from when we played soccer, our legs long and lean and strong, kicking in sharp solid punts. But over the years we have communicated through running—the different pavements and sidewalks and dirt paths and hazy sunrises of so many different towns we've lived in over the years. The years of running, body sleek and strong.

We wear baby oil on smooth skin back in the days when we could soak in the sun, love the feel of warmth seeping in. We wear thin sweatshirts with holes we rip ourselves. We wear white shirts and pants as we march, red vest, white hat with red plume, fingers on a flute that's still cool despite the warm weather, the cadence of the drum beat pounding in our chest, and at the round-off, we pause a beat then blow across the mouthpiece to play a memorized song and move sideways with the rest of the band in synchronized steps.

Every time we wore shoes that were too tight, too high, and we tottered around, propped. Every time we wore jeans flared at the bottom but cinched at the waist. Every time we added silver hoops to the ears, adorned ourselves in scarves and bright blouses, hoping he would notice.

Every whisper heard or not heard. Every email answered or not. Chances taken or lost.

Every time I relinquished a breast to nurse a screaming baby. Every time my body rose to a cry in the night and answered the call before my mind was even aware. Every time my body has tensed in the bleachers, willing the coach to play my child, feeling her sidelined angst in my own bones.

The time we fell on the cobblestone street in Boston, a scar to the knee. The scar on the forehead from a sprinkler thrown by our brother. The scar on the shoulder from removing that mole. The long scar on the lower abdomen, thin and pink and hard, from the C-section that enabled our second daughter's birth.

The scars I don't talk about. The ones that cause the cell memory and keep me in hibernation.

My dear body, how I have burdened you with my fear.

Our bodies house the ghosts of every love and lover. I am scarred from the blurred boundaries around my body, even while I long for touch like a phantom limb.

Fear hibernates in the flesh. The flesh becomes like a cocoon. In the safety of my home I feed my body red wine and fine chocolates by a fire I light for myself. It is a momentary numbing, a thin salve against the loneliness that presses against me like night without moon.

My dear body. How I have taken you for granted.

In theory we are healthy. In theory we eat right and run three miles a day and practice hot yoga and believe in organic believe in recycling believe that beauty starts on the inside. Yet we carry pounds like a cloak of invisibility.

Others have taken my body for granted. As my marriage deteriorates the boundaries of my body blur. I no longer run.

Was it so hard to love, that now I must hide? But the love was easy—that it mutated was hard, so that now my body, containing that cell memory, fears romantic love as trickery. The husband is removed; I sleep alone. What am I afraid of? That I will fall in love, and that love won't be returned? Or worse, that the love will be returned, but that over time it will shift into something not shared but possessed?

How to reclaim faith when the people you love in the world have scarred you? Invited mistresses to dinner; didn't show up on Christmas; didn't call; didn't remember your birthday; remembered your birthday but got you a shitty gift; didn't come to the game; came to the game but left before you went on the field.

I am in a self-imposed exile I consider hibernation. But that implies I will blossom.

We hold the ghosts of every lover, the cell memory of every touch. We crave to feel fingers brush our own, a strong arm surrounding us even in sleep. Even for all the terrible nights. Still, our body yearns.

Every time the first sip of cool wine and the glow of candles and the hum of music as he pulls you up from the wooden chair to dance in the kitchen. Every time you stoop to pick up a penny from the ground, believing it a message from the dead. Every stomach lurch as the plane banks, as the child falls to the pavement, as the coaster, after clicking steadily to the top, finally drops noiselessly down the first steep hill.

Every time you relinquished your body to him.

Every time we drive a road we used to drive, and our body picks up, alert, remembering a place we used to live. And remembering, also, that person we once were, who is still deep inside this body, too.

Every time we lace up our shoes and run.

My dear body, we house the memories, and yet we are in a perpetual state of becoming. Even the hibernation is part of it. We will be the best version of ourselves, someday. Someday.

We cling to hope. We cling to Facebook feeds and fake news and headlines on glossy magazines at the supermarket counter. We cling to loves, our legs wrapped around waists. We cling to the hands of the dying. We promise it will all be okay, but how do we know?

Others have survived what I am trying to survive. And worse. Much worse. Now it is only loneliness, brought on by my self-imposed exile from love. How to find my way back? Am I hibernating or hiding?

I walk with my dog each day and it is one of the purest pleasures I know. She wants nothing but to be outside, to smell the smells. Yet I want everything. I want sights and smells and birdwatching and possibility and a man to snap on white gloves like Captain Von Trapp and books and dreams and a quiet screened porch to rest my body and a deep long pool to stretch and swim.

I want a touch on my cheek again, a hand on my arm as we walk down the path strewn with brown leaves, a canopy of bright green buds, fresh moonlit snow.

My body, there was only one time I felt truly separate from you. It is the time with the miscarriage, and you, my body, wouldn't listen though I begged. On my knees, I begged. You only twisted and roiled and purged. Blood, so much blood.

The time(s) we stepped on a bee. The time(s) we slid it into the purse though we had the money to pay. The time(s) we gave it away because we thought he would love us. The time(s) we stepped into the shower and cried into the water, hoping the kids couldn't hear.

The time, as a teen, we were chased through a dark orchard by a man angry he caught us toilet papering his house. The swishing of the feet through uncut grass, the unseen branches snapping our skin as we ran blindly past.

The times we ran.

What drives me to run again, to regain my body, myself? My writing self is intricately linked to my running self; I learn over the years. It takes time and miles to reclaim, and at first I don't even realize that it's what I'm doing.

Together we run. We run the pavement and dirt paths of every town we've ever lived in. The Aqueduct trail, overlooking the palisades and the Hudson River. The road by the orchard. The trail on the old rail bed that cuts through the woods. The road by the lake.

The beach by the Sound, the breeze from the sea cool on the skin at twenty, when it seemed that life would always have salty breezes from the sea.

The making of lunch for the children, the heating of soup, the shucking of peas. The making of salmon for dinner, yet again. Making love.

When a lover reached out across cotton sheets. When a child reached up in sudden fear. When my grandmother reached out as she was dying, the grip of her hand—thin flesh over bone— surprisingly strong. The cry of my daughter, then a baby, when my grandmother had already slipped from consciousness and that was the one thing that could bring her back—a child's cry. Her body knew, remembered, and woke to answer the call. Opened her eyes and lifted her arms and would not calm until I handed her the child.

We are every name we have ever cried out in passion. We are every name we have ever cried out in grief.

We must own our life. We must cut excuses, and forgo permission from another person—anyone other than you. We must not wait. It is easy to wait until this spring or next, or New Year's Day. It is hard to start now. But that is what we must do.

We must.

We must put on our sneakers, pick up our pens, whatever it is we do, we must carry through the small act of walking that particular path, every day.

Realize that hibernation can be nursed to a crutch. Realize that to wait is to let go.

Action is the only cure for fear. Step forward, again and again, metaphorically and literally. One step at a time can lead you through.

Our bodies remember the motion. They are homesick for joy. We return to the path and they spark up, remember, come alive. They house all that has happened. But they also hold all that we may become.

CONSCIOUSNESS RAISING
Stephanie Ross

Francine Prose wrote an essay "Other Women" published in Granta #115 and then again in *The Best American Essays of 2012*, and I'm to write about it for my writing group. When reading the best essays each year, I know we aren't supposed to compare ourselves, but I do, and unlike many of my fellow writers, I always come to taste envy.

The essay describes how her husband fucked one of the other women in her Consciousness Raising Group. I thought she was brave to write such a piece and I thought she sounded bitter, and angrier with the woman who betrayed her than the man.

I can't understand that. Women have always been embedded in my heart. I loved my mother much more than I loved my father and I loved him deeply. Does everybody lean that way—more mother than father? Still, if my husband had fucked one of the women in my group, I would have wanted to kill them both—but him the most.

I was in a Consciousness Raising Group at Cal Arts. Cal Arts lives outside Valencia, California. My husband had auditioned to be in their acting program and been one of the fourteen out of four zillion to be accepted. The school was built in what once was an orange orchard. When we arrived, my husband and I with our baby, it looked like a hospital. The landscape was parking-lot-bleak and the reason we'd come—Herbert Blau had just quit. We slept in our friend's VW van and walked into an assembly announcing his departure.

We stayed, and I became a student in the Critical Studies section of the Theater Department hoping to finish my BFA, my husband was going for an MFA and I became the dorm mom and created a daycare and a group of women from this daycare formed a Consciousness Raising Group. We always met in the living room of our newly built apartment in the dorms. It was a one bedroom, so we shared the bedroom with the baby and my writing room was in the hall between the living room and the bedroom.

The landscape of Cal Arts breathed desert. I thought all of Southern California would be tropical and jungle and instead it was a landscape pretending to be "not-desert." The fight was always against earthquakes and no water and reality was replaced by make-believe. A big quake had hit Cal Arts months before we arrived and the ground never solidified. Want to be artists are used to instability but Cal Arts cranked it up to a fine art.

Only Cal Arts and the daycare connected the women in the group. We were diverse before it became popular—one woman was black, one Jewish, one Hispanic, and one a Mormon. The remaining three women were white (at least I thought I was but that is another story). And the most beautiful woman fucked the second most beautiful woman's husband like in Francine Prose's essay. I think both betrayals played into a stereotype of women and untrustworthiness. I didn't see it that way. I thought bodies were untrustworthy, that's for sure and that they betray us each and every one.

We sat naked around my living room one night as promised to show each other despicable things about our bodies. We'd been talking about them for weeks—these wretched bodies of ours. We were all in our twenties and had no cause to rake our bodies over such blistering coals, but rake we did. I learned from them that our self-observances were skewed and blurred by some fountain of venom that poured forth from each of our disconnected centers.

Before my husband came home that night, I sat and took a long look in the mirror even doing what *Our Bodies Ourselves* prescribed and looked deep into my own cunt.

Like some Southern flower, I almost blacked out until I felt my consciousness rise like the Northern lights. I was okay. I could choose right then for my body to be imperfectly okay, and I did.

PHOTO READY
Julie Anderson

(34) Bubble Boobs:

My breasts, they are not mine. Well, they are, and they aren't. I bought them when I was 19. Before their arrival, I only sported a pair of nipples.

Being a fashion model, attaining the perfect ten: 34-24-34 is paramount. At the tender age of nineteen, I was 30-24-34. A pear-shaped nothing. So I employed a plastic surgeon who cut them open and inserted a brand new pair of tits. I bought my boobs. Yes I did.

They have been with me for so long that they are mine now. Slowly they are becoming one with my body, a slow leak coursing through my system.

Obviously, I should swap them out for a new set, but the last time I did that I became violently ill immediately after the surgery. Flattened, blue, swollen, wearing a corset of bandages, nauseous, vomiting out my soul for days—not my thing.

My nipples, unfortunately, do not cut it. They point east and west.

I never knew that was a big deal, never even noticed it, until my husband told me so. He said, "Most women's nipples point straight ahead." I have been ashamed of my large eraser-shaped nipples ever since.

(24) Belly Blues:

Here I am seated on the couch, with my laptop at the ready, and my damn belly rolls right over the top of my PJs. If I look at it, which I hate to do, I see cellulite. I am fat with cellulite. There it is, a pouch of ugly. It does not matter that this pouch is the aftermath of giving birth to three babies. I hate it. I feel ugly. I won't wear a bikini because of it. I am never comfortable naked, EVER in front of my husband. My fat cellulite roll screams out, "You are a pig. Stop eating. If you stop eating, the roll will disappear, and the cellulite won't look so bad."

So, every once and a while, I stop eating.

The ramifications of the lack of food are marvelous. I become THIN.

I am told that I look ""great now," and that I am "photo ready."

In my past life, I was a fashion model for many years, and being "photo ready" is Level I. "Photo ready" is a standard that must be maintained on a daily basis. Seriously. I just never know when the phone will ring for a casting, a last-minute gig, whatever. And when you are ready for a photo, you are T H I N.

(34) Thunder Thighs:

My thighs touch. Right there, half an inch down, two crescent shapes emerge. My thighs have decided to kiss. I hate that kiss. Sometimes I stand in front of the mirror and pull my thighs away from each other, just to see what it would look like to have the "gap." And to me, having that gap would be gorgeous. A nice big gap between my legs.

With that gap, I would finally be able to wear the size two Dolce Gabbana slacks that were bought as a gift for me many moons ago. I would wear them and be able to breathe. They would fit perfectly if it were not for that ugly smacking kiss of my thighs. I have been told to work out more on my inner thighs. Work out I have. They never pull away from each other. Maybe I can cut them apart.

My legs are my grandfather's legs. Long, a bit of a knock knee, with a knee cap that looks more like a workman's hat, and ending in thick ankles. They are good traveling legs though. Granddad used to walk for miles. And miles. And miles.

When I walk, I can see waves of cellulite come and go with the tide. I feel its pull. I feel it move. And it's everywhere. Marking my body with pock marked indentations. The fact that I can see it on my legs drives me insane. I don't wear shorts or short skirts because of how ugly my legs are.

If I lose weight, just 10-15 pounds, then I will be able to wear shorts again. And a bikini. And have sex. I will be *photo ready*. Which to me means that I am worthy of love.

THE BODY REMEMBERS
Samantha Paige Rosen

The fall leaves crunch each time Eli hits the ground. It's his first month of kindergarten, and he's already tackling the monkey bars. These particular bars are loops on hinges; they swing when grabbed, making the normally delicate gravitational balance a child must achieve to master monkey bars even harder. Eli puts both hands on the first loop and steps off the platform. He hangs for a few seconds before eating dirt. Because he's a five-year-old boy, he looks up and smiles at me, stands, and grabs the loop again. He falls, gets up again, falls, gets up again, and again, and again, and again, using slightly more finesse in hanging and swinging than he did each time before.

As I watch Eli, I'm reminded of my own monkey bar obsession in elementary school. I came home from school with blisters on my hands from swinging. I'd go forward and backward, one bar at a time and then every other bar. I, too, fell and got up again, and again, and again, and again. Like Eli, I was tiny for my age, and my mom would remark on my relentless pursuit and mastery of this skill.

I decide to try these loops, not hopeful I can swing the way I once could, but eager to show Eli something of my former self. Fingers wrapped around the first loop, I count to three and let my body dangle. Before I let go with my right hand to swing to the next loop, I hear a crunch and feel a pinch in my mid-back that shoots through my spine. I yelp and jump to the ground. This is my body now. Still, I try to recover and race Eli down the slide. As I shimmy from side to side on the way down, my lower back burns.

As we age, many of us experience chronic discomfort. A perpetually stiff neck, a knot in your back that never goes away, a twinge in your knee each time you stand. I'm only 26, but I've been there, too.

There's no real name for what ails me. My primary care doctor calls it "myofascial-myalgia" which is like fibromyalgia, but in one area, with only two trigger points. My most recent orthopedist called it chronic low back pain. My most recent neurologist called it anxiety and depression. My correctional therapist won't call it anything. The name isn't important, he says. What's important is that we can reduce my discomfort. He's probably right. In fact, fibromyalgia is the name given to chronic pain in certain areas of the body without an identifiable cause. It affects an estimated 10 million Americans, 75 to 90 percent of which are women, and 3 to 6 percent globally.

After seven years, four physical therapists, three neurologists, three orthopedists, one doctor of osteopathy, an acupuncturist, a correctional therapist, multiple x-rays, bone scans, MRIs, blood tests, cortisone injections, back braces, and prescriptions for muscle relaxers and anti-inflammatories, there seems to be nothing *really* wrong with me. Nothing shows up on scans. Nothing responds to medication. Doctors examine me and say I'm "a healthy young lady," although I've had chronic back pain since age 19.

I don't feel healthy. I moan in pain when I bend down to put on my socks in the morning. The 10 minutes I stand to put on my makeup causes my back to ache. To compensate for the pressure on my lower back, I have to shift my weight from one foot to the other, which poses a unique challenge to applying eyeliner. I can't walk around a museum or explore New York City for several hours pain-free. My body feels fragile, stiff, sore, and tired. My bones feel heavy. Yet my pain has repeatedly seemed both unidentifiable in cause and resistant to any treatment.

"I believe that the body remembers everything that ever happened to it," writes John F. Barnes, the physical therapist who developed the Myofascial Release Approach. This approach is pseudo-scientific. There are no hard numbers to support it, but it explains a great deal, in my case. Watching Eli, I wonder if the physical and psychological resilience he shows at such a young age could hurt him later on. I want to find out—is this where our bodies start deteriorating? In childhood, where we fall and get up and no one thinks twice about it? When did I start inflicting damage upon mine?

Both musculoskeletal and soft tissue injuries are common in children as they play and grow. Their tissues, muscles, joints, cranial bones, and skeletal bones aren't the same as those of adults. A fall could lead to soft tissue injuries such as bruises, cuts, muscle tears, and scrapes, as well as musculoskeletal injuries like sprains, fractures, and ligament tears. Often these heal by themselves, but if an injury doesn't fully heal, it can have long-term consequences for the body.

Because children are still growing, their bodies can "easily become misaligned... or tight in ways that will affect them as adults," says Marybetts Sinclair, massage therapist and author of *Pediatric Massage Therapy*.

"Scarring and shrinking of connective tissue around injuries," she continues, "can restrict movement and create faulty movement patterns (such as walking with one knee twisted inward to accommodate a frequently sprained ankle). Patterns of muscle tightness can also develop around a single contracted area."

Even something as seemingly benign as learning to stand too soon can have lasting effects on the body. As for the growing pains many of us, myself included, had throughout childhood, Sinclair considers these signs of "chronic discomfort"—an expression of stress in the body.

When I was three, I fell out of a moving stroller and face-planted onto the Atlantic City boardwalk. At 10, I leaned on a shelf that gave out, causing a 75-pound television to bounce off my shoulder and hit the ground with a crack. Could it be that these incidents, from which I emerged emotionally shaken but physically unscathed, actually did hurt me?

According to Sinclair, "Adults often forget events from their childhood and their musculoskeletal adaptations to an accident or injury can become so habitual that by the time they experience a chronic problem, they remember nothing about how it started."

The body remembers what the mind forgets.

Perhaps my chronic pain was determined at birth. I was delivered through caesarean section at two pounds, 10 ounces, jaundiced as a lemon with a double hernia at my pelvis. I was so small the doctors didn't operate on the hernia until I was 10 months old. I spent my first few weeks of life in the NICU in an incubator, like a fuzzy little chick, with a feeding tube through my nose. If I hadn't been in that incubator, I would have died. My system wasn't ready to live outside my mother; I couldn't maintain my own body temperature.

A few days after my birth, I was rushed to the Children's Hospital of Philadelphia to undergo surgery for necrotizing enterocolitis, a common disease affecting preemies where the bowel basically dies. Ultimately, I didn't need the surgery. I did need several blood transfusions, although my parents were never told why.

"We kind of held our breath for the first week or two," my mom remembers. "We weren't sure what was going to be with you. Any little thing can kill a premature baby."

But nothing did. For most of my life, I thought the only side effect of being premature was my small frame and poor vision. It took a few years for my growth and fine motor skills to reach that of other children my age, but otherwise I seemed fine. My digestive system works properly; I have strong lungs, good hearing, and no neurological deficits. But after seven years of back pain, I decided to investigate the effect being born so fragile may have had on my structural development.

Positioning in utero, unusual occurrences during birth or infancy, or any infant injuries can have negative effects on the body throughout a person's life. This is true for all infants, but preemies are unusual by definition. I was born before I had the chance to distinguish pain from touch, which happens around 35 weeks. Additionally, the strange environment in which I spent my first two months of life is stressful on all five senses. As an infant in the NICU, I had blood taken so many times from my heels that I have scar tissue on the bottoms of both my feet. All of this may have made me more sensitive to pain compared to healthy newborns, and even into adulthood.

At nine years old I started dancing ballet. For almost the next decade, I fell completely into a world that demanded everything I had physically, mentally, and emotionally. It quickly became apparent my body wasn't ideal for this art. My feet were flat, I was too curvy, and too muscular in all the wrong places. Most importantly, I had little natural turnout. Turnout comes from the hips and allows the legs to rotate such that the ankles and knees turn to the side. Every position a ballerina takes requires turnout, from pliés at the beginning of class to grand allegro at the end. I could only rotate so much from my hips. To compensate, I faked my turnout by rotating from my knees.

I now realize this put a tremendous amount of pressure on my knees and lower back, but at the time, I only cared about looking like my peers. My teachers knew what I was doing—it was easy to spot, looking at my hips and knees—but no one mentioned how dangerous it was or told me I should stop. No one admonished me for pushing my body past its natural limit. No one taught me how to stretch properly before class, in order to support the movements my body was doing in class. My training was all about daily achievement, proper or safe positions be damned.

Reflecting on his own sports injury, Barnes writes that he "loved competition and motion and had no teachers to tell me 'stop doing that. It's bad for you.'"

This resonates with me, even years after I stopped dancing. I still find myself approaching every new form of exercise and movement as something to be achieved, rather than a process my body must undergo. Growing up with this mindset and having pain as a result seems to be what led us both to myofascial release.

Told last spring by a new neurologist—whom I'd sought out specifically for pain management options—that my anxiety and depression were the cause of my back problems, I resigned myself to doing as he said: noticing my discomfort, but not letting it make me more anxious or depressed.

A fellow sufferer urged me: "Fuck that. Don't give up. Give yourself time and permission to keep searching for the answer."

So I did.

In my experience, doctors can't treat a problem unless they are able to diagnose it. That's where myofascial release is different: it recognizes that while my pain could be caused by any number of things, there are still ways to ease my discomfort. Andrew, my correctional therapist, may never give me a formal diagnosis, but he will always work to lessen my pain.

Myo means muscle. I didn't know what fascia was until this summer when I began my treatment with Andrew. A thick connective tissue that spreads from head to toe without interruption, fascia surrounds every muscle, nerve, bone, blood vessel, and organ. It both supports the structures it surrounds by holding tissues together, and separates these elements to allow for mobility without friction. When injury or inflammation occurs, the fascia thickens in that area to offer even more support. This puts pressure—about 2,000 pounds per square inch, according to Barnes—on everything it surrounds, which can create pain throughout the body, not just in the area where the injury occurred.

Those thousands of pounds of pressure act like a "straitjacket on muscles, nerves, blood vessels and osseous structures producing the symptoms of pain, headaches, restriction of motion, and disease."

Since fascial trauma doesn't show up on X-rays, MRIs, CAT scans, and the like, there's no way of knowing whether my problem is strictly related to fascia. But treating the areas where my fascia is restricted and where there is a tremendous amount of pressure seems to help.

People who have mysterious, undiagnosed pain often have fascial trauma.

Case studies of patients with chronic low back issues like mine all begin more or less the same way: "I have been through all the MRI's, ultrasounds, massages, heat therapy, muscle relaxants, acupuncture, psychiatry, orthopedics, braces, decades of stretching and other exercise at home, etc. etc., all to no avail."

Like me, these people get squirmy driving a car for more than a half hour. I imagine they, too, have cried in the car from the intensity of their pain, and even the luster of lazy days in bed has been tarnished.

After two days, two weeks or, in my case, two months of myofascial release therapy, these people were able to experience life with minimal pain. Now their choices about where to go and how to get there aren't always limited by how their bodies feel. They can drive cars for two hours straight. They can get on planes. They can walk around cities. They can stand at concerts. These are all things I have done since being treated by Andrew.

The goal of myofascial release is to improve the body's structural alignment and reduce abnormal pressure on areas of the body that produce pain. Through myofascial release, soft tissue is freed from the clutch of tight fascia. At each appointment, Andrew evaluates my pain. Wherever he finds my fascia most restricted that day is where he begins. He stretches the muscular component of my fascia so the area is less tight. He applies slow, prolonged pressure to the most sensitive areas. This is a mild touch. He holds the fascial area that's restricted for several minutes, until he can gain access to the deeper layer of fascia. Ideally, what will happen next is something called "resonance," or release of fascial tension.

Since Andrew reevaluates me each time we have a session, he typically ends up using a combination of myofascial release, massage, and structural work. What seems to help me feel relief the fastest and for the longest amount of time is when I lie on my side and he gently stretches the skin across my spine with both of his hands, holding pressure on my most painful spots.

Myofascial release is supposed to allow the body's natural healing capacity to function properly. I have felt this only slightly. I saw Andrew for seven weeks before noticing any difference. In that time, I wavered between feelings of hope derived from Andrew's optimism, and complete despair when I felt no difference in my pain each week.

After our seventh appointment, in early August, I drove three hours to Washington D.C. for a long weekend. I prepared myself, physically, mentally and emotionally to hurt. I wore a back brace in the car. I took ibuprofen before my car ride and before a day of walking around the city. I brought the special ice packs Andrew gave me and stored them in my friend's freezer. I reminded myself that my back would probably feel worse from this car ride, walking so much, and sleeping on my friend's second-hand sofa bed. Yet the pain didn't come. I felt some stiffness from the car, but after ten minutes sitting against an ice pack, it went away. The rest of the weekend, my body felt like it used to. I couldn't believe it.

Since then, my pain has been less severe. On a scale of 0 to 10, I used to wake up at a five or sometimes even a seven. Now, I usually write .5 to 1.5 in my daily back pain journal.

After one more session with Andrew, I returned to New York for my second year of graduate school. I would have continued to see him on a weekly basis had I stayed in Philadelphia. I've read the longer a person's pain has been present, the longer it takes to resolve the problem. Some chronic conditions take three or four months of treatments several times a week to achieve the best results. Should I have seen Andrew twice a week? He said it wasn't necessary, and I couldn't really afford it, but the internet consensus seems to be the more intensive myofascial treatment a person gets, the better off they are. Someday, I might amp up my myofascial release therapy to several times per week so I can once and for all get rid of my pain. Or maybe that's wishful thinking.

I'm seeing Andrew next week for the first time in almost three months. I wonder what state he will find my back in. I've tried to take all he has taught me to New York, making changes to my physical habits, stretching and moving more, drinking more water, and breathing deliberately. Equally important, I learned from Andrew that drastic changes also needed to be applied to my mental and emotional states.

Throughout my childhood, my dad repeated, "Life is a journey, not a destination" and other related clichés. He never said this to my sisters; even at a young age, he saw my tendency toward perfectionism, achievement, and end result, which mirrored his own. The deep

237

breathing, quiet mind, and overall relaxation Andrew required of Type-A me, lying still in my underwear for our hour-long appointments, took some getting used to. But after two months, I could see he had succeeded in showing me how to focus on the present moment in a way no family member or psychologist had (incidentally, Andrew used to be a psychotherapist). These qualities suddenly mattered a great deal because he connected them to my physical trauma. My habits now, both mental and physical, are better overall.

Knowing what I know now about the body, I see potential structural danger everywhere I look. I notice, in particular, a picture of my friend's toddler hitting a piñata for the first time. Stepping forward with his left foot, back with his right, little Miles holds the bat with his dad's help. It's his neck, head, and jaw I'm watching. His head is thrown back about 15 degrees, eyes toward the sky, mouth open as wide as can be. To judge from this picture, this is the happiest moment of Miles' life. But is it possible this stance, repeated too often, or even this one time, could hurt him later on? As he grows up, the key is to learn how to become mindful of his body and to relax.

"Remember," Andrew wrote to me recently, "there are no 100 percent answers to your pain, just possibilities and dynamic shifts that have impacted multiple layers of tissue over time."

THE END:

All those scars and scabs. All those dimples in the thigh.

It's all a poem to me.

Acknowledgements

The editors would like to thank the following winners of the *My Body, My Words* #sixwordmemoir contest in collaboration with *Smith Magazine*:

"Dear marrow: I'll never forgive you."
—@KathrynDiPasqua

"I'm taking away your self-destruct button."
—@Sammie_Grace

"My physical strength keeps surprising me."
—mariposa

"Wrinkles narrate my body of work."
—FKA_Liza

"Dear body: don't act your age."
—canadafreeze

"These scars represent my many blessings."
—brokenlens

The editors would also like to acknowledge the following organizations, supporters, and partners of the *My Body, My Words* project for their championship:

Chenese Lewis, Host and Creator, Chenese Lewis Show. Learn more at http://www.cheneselewis.com.

Elena Rossini, Filmmaker, *The Illusionists*, "a powerful, critically acclaimed documentary about the globalization of beauty. Our mission: to spark a body image revolution." Learn more at https://theillusionists.org.

Feminine Collective who "publishes original stories from new, emerging and established writers and poets. These are unique human interest stories not found in mainstream media." Learn more at https://www.femininecollective.com.

Our Front Cover: Stories of unsung heroes, social entrepreneurs, start -ups, artists, conservationist, writers and musicians. Stories of change makers, out of box thinkers and restless souls who believe in shaking up the society. Learn more at http://ourfrontcover.com.

Six-Word Memoirs of Smith Magazine, including Larry Smith, Shauna Healey Greene, and Jonathan Zipper for their collaboration in the #MyBodyMySixWords Contest.

Unpolished Journey, "an organization dedicated to helping transform lives by cultivating a space that focuses on three elements: community, creativity, and spirituality." Learn more at https://unpolishedjourney. org.

Robin Stratton, for your patience, encouragement, and unwavering support.

Martha Frankel, for lending your amazing voice.

About the Editors

Amye Archer holds an MFA in Creative Nonfiction from Wilkes University. Her memoir, *Fat Girl, Skinny,* was named runner-up for the Red Hen Press Nonfiction Manuscript Award and was released in April, 2016, by Big Table Publishing Company. She has two poetry collections: *BANGS* and *A Shotgun Life*, both published by Big Table Publishing. Amye's work has appeared in *Brevity, Hippocampus, Mothers Always Write, Nailed Magazine, PMS: Poem Memoir Story, PANK*, and *Provincetown Arts*. Her Essay, "Slow Motion," received a notable in *Best American Essays 2016*. Amye is a regular contributor to *Feminine Collective* and is the creator of *The Fat Girl Blog*.

Loren Kleinman is a faculty member at New York Writer's Workshop and a full-time freelance writer and social media strategist. Her poetry has appeared in *The New York Times*, ADANNA, *Drunken Boat, The Moth, Domestic Cherry, Blue Lake Review, Columbia Journal, LEVURE LITTÉRAIRE, Nimrod, Wilderness House Literary Review, Narrative Northeast, Writer's Bloc, Journal of New Jersey Poets, Paterson Literary Review (PLR), Resurgence (UK), HerCircleEzine* and *Aesthetica Annual*. Her interviews appeared in *IndieReader, USA Today*, and *The Huffington Post*. She's also published essays in *Cosmopolitan, Good Housekeeping*, and *Seventeen Magazine*. She is the author of *Flamenco Sketches* and *Indie Authors Naked*, which was an Amazon Top 100 bestseller in Journalism in the UK and USA. Kleinman's *The Dark Cave Between My Ribs* was named one the best poetry books of 2014 by *Entropy Magazine*. Her third collection of poetry *Breakable Things* released via Winter Goose Publishing in March 2015. Her novel *This Way to Forever* released August 2016, and her memoir, *The Woman with a Million Hearts* released April 2016 via BlazeVOX. *Stay with Me Awhile* is her fourth collection of poetry.

About the Contributors

Vicki Addesso co-authored the collaborative memoir *Still Here Thinking of You~A Second Chance with Our Mothers* (Big Table Publishing, 2013).

Julie Anderson is the creator and publisher of FeminineCollective.com, a literary magazine with bite. In addition to the magazine, Julie is also the Publisher of Feminine Collective Media, a boutique publishing house. A survivor of her reign as a 90's Supermodel, she considers herself incredibly lucky to have found her "voice."

Renée Ashley is the author of six volumes of poetry: *The View from the Body* (Black Lawrence Press), *Because I Am the Shore I Want to Be the Sea* (Subito Book Prize, University of Colorado—Boulder); *Basic Heart* (X.J.Kennedy Poetry Prize, Texas Review Press); *The Revisionist's Dream; The Various Reasons of Light;* and *Salt* (Brittingham Prize in Poetry, University of Wisconsin Press), as well as a novel, *Someplace Like This,* and two chapbooks, *The Museum of Lost Wings* (Hill-Stead Museum) and *The Verbs of Desiring* (new american press). She has received fellowships in both poetry and prose from the New Jersey State Council on the Arts and a fellowship in poetry from the National Endowment of the Arts. A portion of her poem, "First Book of the Moon," is included in a permanent installation by the artist Larry Kirkland in Penn Station, NYC. She has served as Assistant Poetry Coordinator for the Geraldine R. Dodge Foundation and as Poetry Editor of *The Literary Review*. Ashley teaches in the low-residency MFA in Creative Writing and the MA in Creative Writing and Literature for Educators programs at Fairleigh Dickinson University. She lives in northern New Jersey.

Jayme Beddingfield is a freelance writer and podcaster. She has been crafting stories since her third-grade assignment to write her own fairy tale. Some are about mystical lands. Some are about antiheroes on the road to redemption. Some are about neither. She is host and producer of *Too Many Words,* an interview podcast with a focus on creating and how it feels. She prefers to work near brick walls with her dogs by her feet. Originally from Northern New Jersey, she now lives in Seattle, the city of her dreams. She lives with her husband, two children, and pack of dogs. Jayme is a supporter of dreams and promoter of kindness.

Ali Beemsterboer earned her MFA from Western Washington University. Her writing lends extra attention to bodily experiences. Her work has appeared in Jeopardy Magazine, Suffix Webzine, and Poplorish.

Paula Bomer is the author of the collection, *Inside Madeleine* (Soho Press, May 2014), the novel *Nine Months* (Soho Press, August 2012), which received exuberant reviews in *The Atlantic, Publishers Weekly, Library Journal, The Minneapolis Star Tribune* and elsewhere. Her collection, *Baby and Other Stories* (Word Riot Press, December 2010), received a starred review in *Publishers Weekly*, calling it a "lacerating take on marriage and motherhood…not one to share with the Mommy and Me group", *Kirkus Review* deemed it "a worthy, if challenging, entry into the genre of transgressional fiction", and O *Magazine* referred to it as a "brilliant, brutally raw debut." Links to various work, interviews and more can be found here. She also is the publisher of Sententia Books and edits Sententia: The Literary Journal.

Emily Blair is the Director of Operations of Unpolished Journey (unpolishedjourney.org), an organization run by her and her sister, Morgan, which seeks to create a community for those in recovery. She currently attends Loyola University of Chicago, in which she is studying Human Services, Education Policy, and Spanish. She also has a deep love for karate, as it has become a large part of her personal recovery journey. She believes it is a way to build up a spirit of empowerment.

Morgan Blair is the Founder and Creative Director of Unpolished Journey, which is a community of individuals sharing their recovery journeys through art, writing, and community outreach. She is a Chicago based artist who paints personalized wall tapestries and canvases based on words that are inspirational for those receiving the artwork. Aside from painting and writing, she loves scuba diving, traveling, and watching good films.

Dana Boyer graduated with her MA in Creative Writing from the University of Nebraska in 2010, and has been traveling the world since. She has published poetry in places like A Clean, Well-Lighted Place and the Tishman Review, and occasionally publishes parenting articles in order to convince herself she is grounded in Real Life. She currently lives in Florida with her family, and is never too far from a beach.

Sarah Bregel is a mother, a writer, and deep-breather based in Baltimore, Maryland. She has contributed to *The Washington Post*, *New York Magazine*, *Good Housekeeping*, *Vice*, *Vox*, *The Establishment*, and *Parents Magazine*. She is working on her first book, a memoir about untimely motherhood.

Lillian Bustle is a burlesque performer, singer, MC, and public speaker/gleeful loudmouth about body love! Her recent TEDx talk, *Stripping Away Negative Body Image*, sheds light on the positive effect of burlesque and visual diet on self-image, and her message has been shared by millions of people worldwide. She can be heard co-hosting *The Body PosCast* with actress and activist Liza Poor. Find out more at www.lillianbustle.com.

Lily Caraballo is a candidate of the MFA Creative Writing Program at Antioch University in Los Angeles. She is a staff member of the school's online literary journal, *Lunch Ticket* and a West Coast Correspondent for *Black Girl Nerds*. When not writing, Lily works as a figure model for the University of Southern California and El Camino College.

Hélène Cardona's recent books include *Life in Suspension, Dreaming My Animal Selves*, the translations *Birnam Wood, Beyond Elsewhere*, winner of a Hemingway Grant, *Ce que nous portons*, and Walt Whitman's *Civil War Writings*. She contributes to *The London Magazine, World Literature Today, Washington Square Review,* and *Poetry International* among many, and co-edits *Plume* and *Levure Littéraire*. She judged the 2017 Jacar Press Full Length Competition, the 2016 PEN Center USA Translation Award, the 2015 Writer's Digest Challenge, the 2014 Rabindranath Tagore Award, and received fellowships from the Goethe-Institut and Universidad Internacional de Andalucía. She won the 2017 International Book Award in Poetry, the 2017 Best Book Award in Poetry, the USA Best Book Award, 2 Pinnacle Book Awards for Best Bilingual Poetry Book, and 2 Readers' Favorite Book Awards.

Jennifer Kircher Carr's fiction has been nominated for the Pushcart Prize, and is published in numerous literary journals, including *The*

Rumpus, North American Review, Monkeybicycle, Prairie Schooner, Hobart, Alaska Quarterly, Jellyfish Review, and *The Nebraska Review,* where it also won the Fiction Prize. Her non-fiction is published in *Ploughshares* online, North American Review online, and Poets & Writers, among others. She is currently working on a novel and a collection of linked fiction.

Wynn Chapman's essays have appeared in *Blackbird, CutBank,* and *The James Franco Review.* The title piece of her memoir, "The War of the Ashes," was selected as a Notable Essay/Literary Nonfiction piece in Best American Essays 2016. An earlier version of this essay first appeared in *CutBank* 82 (2015). She lives with her spouse in Kentucky.

Tyler Dibble is a freshman at Central Michigan University and has held writing close to her for many years. She has been interviewed by *Electric Poetry* and her works have been used by *Every Woman's Place.* Her biggest writing accomplishment was being the 2017 *SHOWCASE* Literary winner for her poetry.

Beverly Donofrio's memoir, the New York Times bestseller, *Riding in Cars with Boys,* was made into a movie. *Looking for Mary* and *Astonished* are much praised, as are her three picture books; the latest, *Where's Mommy,* was a New York Times Best Children's Book; her essays are widely anthologized and appear in *The New York Times, Washington Post, Los Angeles Times, O, The Oprah Magazine, Marie Clair, More, Allure, Spirituality and Health, Huffington Post, Slate.*

Brian Fanelli still watches horror movies and likes writing about them. He is the author of the poetry collections *Waiting for the Dead to Speak* (NYQ Books) and *All That Remains* (Unbound Content), as well as the chapbook *Front Man* (Big Table Publishing). His poetry, essays, and book reviews have been published by *The Los Angeles Times, World Literature Today, The Paterson Literary Review, Main Street Rag, Louisiana Literature, Verse Daily,* and elsewhere. His poetry has also been featured on "The Writer's Alamance" with Garrison Keillor. He has an M.F.A. from Wilkes University and a Ph.D. from SUNY Binghamton. Currently, he teaches at Lackawanna College.

Jason Fjord is a trans student living and writing in New York. Fjord's been published in *Phoenix Magazine*, *The Golden Wave Newspaper*, and the local *Herald*.

Eve Fox lives in upstate NY where she and her husband are raising two sons and taking care of an enormous garden. When she's not helping non-profit organizations use the Internet to recruit supporters, raise money and change the world for the better, she writes about growing, foraging for, cooking and eating good food. You can read more on her blog: http://www.thegardenofeating.org

The only job **Martha Frankel** has ever had is "writer", which makes her completely unemployable! She is the host of *Woodstock Booktalk*, a weekly radio show/podcast that highlights books and authors, and the executive director of the yearly book orgy, Woodstock Bookfest. She would most often rather be knitting.

Megan Culhane Galbraith is a fellow of The Saltonstall Foundation and The Virginia Center for the Creative Arts. Her work received a Notable in Best American Essays 2017, edited by Leslie Jamison. Her essays are published in *Longreads*, *The Coachella Review*, *Catapult*, *PANK*, *Beyond*, *Hotel Amerika*, among others. She is Associate Director the Bennington Writing Seminars.

Marisa Gershenhorn is an illustrator and animator from New York City. She attended Hampshire College, and recently completed her thesis film, an animated short called *The End of Inertia*. Her work includes illustration for concert posters, packaging, and T-shirt designs, as well as animation for Hubbub Inc. productions such as Dear Trump Voter. She has three pet snails. Follow her work at www.marisagershenhorn.com.

Katie Grudens Graduating from Ithaca College about a year ago, Katherine Grudens is coping with all of the changes that adulthood brings and finds that words truly are the doors to support and self-expression. She has moved back home again with her parents and twin sister on Long Island, NY and has used this time to get published via *Feminine Collective*. In the future, she hopes to continue writing, build a career and bring light to everything she does.

Kathleen McKitty Harris is a native New Yorker whose essays and humor have appeared in *Creative Nonfiction, McSweeney's, The Rumpus, Full Grown People,* and *Vela Magazine,* among others. She has also performed as a storyteller at The Moth in New York City, and at the "Listen To Your Mother" live-reading series in northern New Jersey, where she lives with her husband and two children. Follow Kathleen on Twitter @kmckharris.

Aimee Herman is a Brooklyn-based performance artist, poet, and teacher. Aimee has two full-length books of poems, most recently *meant to wake up feeling* (great weather for MEDIA).

Pamela Hughes graduated from Brooklyn College with an MFA in Creative Writing. Her eco-themed book of poems, *Meadowland Take My Hand,* was released in 2017 by Three Mile Harbor Press, New York. She is the editor of Narrative Northeast, a literary and arts magazine that supports diverse voices and visions, including feminist voices, and the environment. For more, visit: www. narrativenortheast.com and www.pamelahugheswrites.com. Read her gynocentric inspired poem, "Vote Bush" online at *PANK Magazine*: www.pankmagazine.com.

Lucas Hunt is a celebrated American poet and the president of HUNT Auctioneers, who was born and raised in rural Iowa. His work has been published in *The New York Times,* and received The John Steinbeck Award for Poetry. He is the author of *IOWA, Light on the Concrete,* and *Lives.* Lucas has helped raise millions of dollars and awareness for non-profit organizations. He graduated from World Wide College of Auctioneering, holds the coveted Benefit Auctioneer Specialist (BAS) designation, and is an outstanding member of the National Auctioneer's Association. He lives in New York.

Kaylie Jones is the author of *Lies My Mother Never Told Me,* a Publishers Weekly starred review memoir chosen as one of the hottest summer reads by *The Palm Beach Pulse, The Daily Beast,* and *The Pittsburgh Post Gazette.* Kaylie was born in Paris, France and attended French schools until she returned with her family to the U.S. in 1974. Her father was the novelist James Jones.

Heather Lang, a poet, writer, and literary critic, was voted Las Vegas' 2017 Best Local Writer or Poet by the readers of KNPR's *Desert Companion*. Her poetry and prose have been published by or are forthcoming with *The Normal School, Paper Darts, Pleiades, South Dakota Review*, and elsewhere. In 2017, she curated *Legs of Tumbleweeds, Wings of Lace: An Anthology of Literature by Nevada Women*, which was funded, in part, by the Nevada Arts Council and the National Endowment for the Arts. Heather serves as World Literature Editor for *The Literary Review*. She holds an MFA in Poetry with a certificate in Literary Translation from Fairleigh Dickinson University, and she works as Adjunct Faculty Coordinator for Nevada State College where she also teaches Composition and Asian Literature, among other courses. www.heatherlang.cassera.net

Dawn Leas is the author of a full-length collection, *Take Something When You Go*, (Winter Goose Publishing 2016), and a chapbook, *I Know When to Keep Quiet*, (Finishing Line Press, 2010). Her poems have appeared in *Literary Mama, Southern Women's Review, San Pedro River Review, The Pedestal Magazine* and elsewhere. She won an honorable mention in the 2005 Dorothy Sargent Rosenberg Poetry Prize and was nominated for a Pushcart Prize. Find out more at www.dawnleas.com.

Bryne Lewis is a writer and thinker, creating and facilitating in Northeastern Central PA. Bryne earned a Masters in Theology from the University of Scranton and teaches philosophy at Luzerne County Community College. Her poetry has been featured in several publications including *Janus Head: Journal of Interdisciplinary Studies* and *The Anglican Theological Review*. Bryne also comments on culture at norvillerodgers.com. She is currently wrestling a collection of essays on parenting and gender to completion.

Monique Antonette Lewis is an annual reader for the James Jones First Novel Fellowship. A former board member of the New York Writers Workshop, she taught fiction workshops in Manhattan and Brooklyn. She was also the fiction editor for *City Lit Rag*. She has more than a decade of journalism experience and is an editor for *Mergermarket*, a global online financial news service. Her articles have appeared in *Forbes* and the *Financial Times*. Prior to *Mergermarket*, Monique was a reporter for the *Press & Sun-Bulletin* (Binghamton, NY) and *The Daily Times* (Salisbury, Md.) She received her MFA in Creative

Writing from Wilkes University, and a B.A. in Journalism from Colorado State University. Monique lives in Denver.

Lucy M. Logsdon resides in Southern Illinois where she raises chickens, ducks & other creatures with her husband & two rebel stepgrrls. A Best of the Net, Pushcart, and Forward Poetry Prize nominee, her work has appeared or is forthcoming in numerous places, including: *Nimrod, Heron Tree, Poet Lore, Rust+Moth, Seventeen, Crack the Spine, Literary Orphans, Talking Writing, Gingerbread, Five 2 One, RightHandPointing* and *Pure Slush: Freak*. Her chapbook, *The Burning Girl*, will appear soon.

Katharina Love is a retired psychotherapist turned blogger. You can find her blog at thefatjewess.wordpress.com. Katharina lives in Toronto with her beloved puppy Lucille.

Rachel Mans McKenny has been published in *The Knee Jerk Review, Shadows, Tenth Muse*, and forthcoming in the *Sandy River Review*, as well as the anthology *The Way WeSleep*. Her essays have been published in *The Chronicle of Higher Education* and forthcoming in *US Catholic and Mothers Always Write*. She's a lecturer at Iowa State University.

Katie McBroom is the award-winning blogger of Martinis and Mascara, a lifestyle blog devoted to beauty, booze, fashion, food, and fun. Martinis and Mascara gained national recognition when Katie was selected as a finalist in *Allure* Magazine's 2013 Beauty Blogger Awards. She eluded elimination in all five rounds of the contest and was ultimately dubbed the Most Buzzworthy Blogger of the Year for producing the most viral content across multiple social media platforms. Since then, she's garnered media attention in multiple publications including *Refinery 29, Buzzfeed, NewBeauty, Health*, and *Seventeen*. Babble selected Katie as one of the 10 best beauty bloggers in the prestigious *Babble 100*. Katie was also dubbed one of the "5 beauty bloggers you need to follow" by Giuliana Rancic's *FabFitFun* and chosen as one of *Lucky Magazine's* New Voices of Beauty. Additionally, Katie has gained international acclaim and was named one of the best beauty bloggers in the world by *White Horse Digital* and has been featured in *Marie Claire Taiwan*.

Marissa McNamara teaches English composition and creative writing at Georgia State University where she also a reader *for The Chattahoochee Review*. She writes drama, short stories, poetry, and essays. Her work has appeared in several publications the journals *RATTLE*, *Assisi*, *Melancholy Hyperbole*, *StorySouth*, *Future Cycle*, *The Cortland Review*, *The Amsterdam Quarterly*, and *First Weekly Review*. Marissa credits the finding of her "voice" to Women Writing for a Change in Cincinnati, Ohio. She lives in Atlanta with her two crazy dogs, her very patient boyfriend, and a flock of pink plastic flamingos.

Lis Mesa was born in Havana, Cuba, raised in Miami, Florida and is currently pursuing a MSc in Creative Writing at the University of Edinburgh, Scotland where she is working on her first novel.

Zorida Mohammed is a Trinidadian-American poet. She is an active member of the Red Wheel Barrow Poets in Rutherford, NJ and reads regularly in NJ and NY. She won a NJ State Council on the Arts grant for poetry in 1991-92 for the manuscript *Shantytown*. Publications include *Fulcrum #6* and *#7*, Phoebe, *The Dirty Goat*, *Atlanta Review*, *The Caribbean writer*, *Oyez Review*, *The Spoon River Poetry Review*, *Quercus Review*, *Bayou. the Rutherford Red Wheelbarrow* and other publications. She's been social worker/therapist for the past 29 years.

Amber Moore is a PhD student at the University of British Columbia studying language and literacy education with the Faculty of Education. Her research interests include adolescent literacy, trauma literature, and exploring gender and sexualities issues in school. She also enjoys writing poetry and creative nonfiction. You can email her at amberjanellemoore@gmail.com

Dinty W. Moore is author of numerous books. He has been published in *The Southern Review, The Georgia Review, Harpers, The New York Times Sunday Magazine, The Philadelphia Inquirer Magazine, Gettysburg Review, Utne Reader, Crazyhorse*, and *Okey-Panky*, among numerous other venues. Dinty lives in Athens, Ohio and teaches a crop of brilliant undergraduate and stunningly talented graduate students as director of Ohio University's BA, MA, and PhD in Creative Writing program.

Jennifer Morgan is an amateur writer and very excited to be welcomed into this collective. She is also a daughter, sister, wife, aunt, friend, cat-mom, and cubicle farmer. Jennifer tries to find humor in every situation and her native language is sarcasm. She loves to travel and hopes her future will reside Oceanside.

s. Nicholas teaches high school in the San Bernardino Mountains where she lives with her three children and one husband. She has a BA in English/World Literature and Psychology from Pitzer College, as well as a Master's in Education from Claremont Graduate University. She also has an MFA in Creative Writing from Cal State San Bernardino. Her work has appeared, or is forthcoming, in *Gesture, Tin Cannon, The Smoking Poet, Sugared Water, Two Words For, Inlandia: A Literary Journey, Amethyst Arsenic, Words Dance, the anthology Orangelandia: The Literature of Inland Citrus*, and the anthology *All We Can Hold: poems of motherhood*.

Karol Neilson is the author of the memoir, *Black Elephants* (Bison Books, 2011), and the poetry chapbook, *This Woman I Thought I'd Be* (Finishing Line Press, 2012). Her memoir was shortlisted for the William Saroyan International Prize for Writing in nonfiction in 2012. Excerpts were honored as Notable Essays in *The Best American Essays* in 2010 and 2005. Her work has appeared in *The Moment Anthology* and many publications. She teaches writing at New York Writers Workshop.

Molly Pennington writes columns, commentary and criticism in print and online. Her work often focuses on the intersections of popular culture, social justice and feminism. She also writes on parenting and relationships. She has essays published or forthcoming in several anthologies and is at work on her memoir—about her estranged father, his performance art suicide, and the mess he left behind.

Eloísa Pérez-Lozano is a long-distance member of the Latino Writers Collective in Kansas City. Two of her poems were finalists in the 2017 Friendswood Public Library Ekphrastic Poetry contest. A 2016 Sundress Publications Best of the Net nominee, her poetry has been featured in *The Texas Observer, Houston Chronicle*, and *The Acentos Review*, among others. She lives with her family in Houston, Texas.

Jared Povanda is a writer of fiction and nonfiction from Horseheads, New York. He graduated Summa cum laude from Ithaca College with a degree in Writing in 2017, and his time in Ithaca exposed him to many different genres, authors, and a healthy fear of steep hills. You can find him curled up on the couch with a good book or sitting by the window writing one of his own. Follow him on Twitter @JaredPovanda.

Francesca Rendle-Short is an award-winning novelist, memoirist and essayist. She is author of the novel *Imago* and critically acclaimed memoir-cum-novel *Bite Your Tongue*, and co-editor of the recent anthology *The Near and The Far*, a collection of work from 21 of the best writers in the Asia-Pacific region. Her work has appeared in anthologies, literary journals, academic journals, online and in exhibitions including *Best Australian Science Writing*, *Killing the Buddha*, *The Lifted Brow*, *Just Between Us* (Pan Macmillan), *Overland, Bumf, Rabbit, Margaret Lawrence Gallery, Queensland Historical Atlas, New Writing, Life Writing* and *The Essay Review* (Iowa). Her artwork is in the collection of the Queensland State Library. She is an associate professor at RMIT University, founder and co-director of non/fictionLab and WrICE (Writers Immersion and Cultural Exchange). She has a Doctor of Creative Arts from the University of Wollongong, and was the recipient of an International Nonfiction Writer's Fellowship at the University of Iowa, USA in 2013. She lives in Melbourne Australia.

Samantha Paige Rosen earned her MFA in Creative Nonfiction from Sarah Lawrence College, where she was too afraid to write about herself for the entire first semester. She has written and edited for newspapers, magazines, television shows, nonprofit organizations, communications firms, colleges and universities, and more. Samantha's bylines include *The Washington Post, Ms. Magazine, The Week, The Philadelphia Inquirer, Bustle, The Huffington Post, Hypertext Magazine, The Passed Note, Beautiful Minds Magazine,* and *Attn.* She recently began hosting a monthly writers' workshop in the Washington D.C. area, and hopes to surround herself with a community of brilliant, big-hearted storytellers wherever she may live.

Stephanie Ross's plays include *Medea Now!* (read at LATC and performed as one of three works selected for staged readings at the Ivy Substation), *Life After Life & Crazy Quilt* (performed at the Seattle Center by the Hard Times Theater Company), *Coming of Age in Gomorrah* (Cornish Institute in Seattle in collaboration with Allied Arts),

Unveiling the Evolutionary Landscape (funded by the Seattle Arts Commission), *Images of Supremacy* (funded by a grant from the Washington State Council for the Humanities), and others. Stephanie Ross received her B.F.A. from California Institute of the Arts. She was the recipient of a King County Arts Commission Written Works-in-Progress grant. She is currently a member of the Dramatists Guild and PEN International. Stephanie Ross spent some twenty-five years working in late night television for *The Tonight Show starring Johnny Carson* and *The Tonight Show with Jay Leno*. She retired as Producer in 2012.

Ryan K. Sallans, MA is a public speaker and author specializing in health care, higher ed, and workplace inclusion for the LGBTQ community. Ryan's memoir, *Second Son: Transitioning Toward My Destiny, Love and Life* has been noted as required reading in Mary Karr's NYT Bestselling book, *The Art of Memoir*. Ryan has appeared on numerous talk shows, including two appearances on *Larry King Live*. He is currently working on his second book.

Susan Shapiro, an award-winning writing professor, freelances for *The New York Times, New York Magazine, Wall Street Journal, Washington Post, L.A. Times, Newsweek, Elle, Esquire* and *Oprah.com*. She's the New York Times bestselling author of 11 books, including the acclaimed memoirs *Lighting Up, Only as Good as Your Word,* and *Five Men Who Broke My Heart*, the coauthored nonfiction books *Unhooked* and *The Bosnia List*, and the novel *What's Never Said*. She and her husband, a TV/film writer, live in Greenwich Village, where she teaches her popular "instant gratification takes too long" classes at the New School, NYU and in private workshops and seminars.

Kitty Sheenan Writer and editor Kitty Sheehan is a former elementary teacher, corporate trainer, consignment store owner and graphic designer. A native Iowan and graduate of the University of Iowa, Kitty founded and directs the Dartbrook Writers Retreat. A freelance copywriter, she is also a social media editor and consultant for several brands. Kitty edits manuscripts and essays for writers of all genres. She is editorial director for the annual Woodstock Bookfest in Woodstock, NY, and a regular workshop teacher at the event. Kitty's essay, "Irish Wake-up Call" appears in the anthology *Shades of Blue*, edited by Amy Ferris, published by Seal Press, 2015. A resident of the

Hudson Valley, Kitty is a past contributor to Hudson Valley magazine. Visit her website at kittysheehan.com and find her on Twitter at @KittyASheehan.

Robin Stratton has been a writing coach in the Boston area for over 20 years. She is the Senior Editor of *Boston Literary Magazine*, Acquisitions Editor at Big Table Publishing Company, and the Director of the Newton Writing and Publishing Center. She is also the author of four novels, including one which was a National Indie Excellence Book Award finalist, two collections of poetry and short fiction, and a writing guide. A four-time Pushcart Prize nominee, she's been published in *Word Riot, 63 Channels, Antithesis Common, Poor Richard's Almanac(k), Blink-Ink, Pig in a Poke, Chick Flicks, Up the Staircase, Shoots and Vines*, and many others. She'd love to have you visit her at www.robinstratton.com

Heidi Stuber spends her days at a homemade treadmill desk and her free time as a warrior and neurodiversity advocate. She began her adult life studying spider monkeys in Costa Rica, later downgrading to the study of human behavior in office environments. She was recently published for the first time in *Unbroken Journal*. Heidi lives in Seattle with her red-headed son and their murderous menagerie.

Abigail Thomas, the daughter of renowned science writer Lewis Thomas (*The Lives of a Cell*), is the mother of four children and the grandmother of twelve. Her academic education stopped when, pregnant with her oldest daughter, she was asked to leave Bryn Mawr during her first year. She's lived most of her life on Manhattan's Upper West Side, and was for a time a book editor and for another time a book agent. Then she started writing for publication. Her first three books, *Getting Over Tom, An Actual Life*, and Herb's *Pajamas* were works of fiction. Her memoir, *A Three Dog Life*, was named one of the best books of 2006 by the *Los Angeles Times* and *The Washington Post*. It won the 2006 Inspirational Memoir Award given by *Books for A Better Life*. She is also author of *Safekeeping*, a memoir, and *Thinking About Memoir*. She lives in Woodstock, New York, with her dogs.

Ashley Nell Tipton, Winner of *Project Runway*, 24, was born and raised in San Diego, California. The youngest of four children she had an early passion for fashion. Tipton remembers discovering her love of sewing when she would design clothes for her Barbies. She learned to sew on her grandmother's sewing machine when she was just seven years old. She won challenges and became a fan favorite on the show. She won her season of *Project Runway* and won even more praise. Now, she is living her mission and making full figured fashion for women and using her win on *Project Runway* and making a real impact for people who want a bit more color and a bit more boldness in their closets and wardrobes. Ashley is currently working on making fashion fun and funky with partnerships with JC Penney and Sally Beauty Supply.

Leah Vernon is a twenty-something African-American Muslim from Detroit. She's an indie author who's just published her first speculative fiction novel, *Impure* (Amazon). Her main focus is bringing diversity to commercial YA/NA fiction. She has a B.S. in management, an M.A. in creative writing/fiction, and an MFA in publishing from Wilkes University. When she isn't writing or eating tasty foods, she's modeling and tending to her body positive style blog *Beauty and the Muse*.

Jim Warner's poetry has appeared in various journals including *The North American Review, RHINO Poetry, New South*, and is the author of two collections (PaperKite Press). His third collection, *Actual Miles*, will be released in 2018 by Sundress Publications. Jim is the host of the literary podcast Citizen Lit and is a faculty member of Arcadia University's MFA program.

E. R. Zhang is a tiny post-graduate student who mostly writes LGBT-themed fiction.